Writing

RICHARD ASHDOWNE

JAMES MORWOOD

Bloomsbury Academic
An imprint of Bloomsbury Publishing Plc

B L O O M S B U R Y
LONDON • NEW DELHI • NEW YORK • SYDNEY

Bloomsbury Academic

An imprint of Bloomsbury Publishing Plc

50 Bedford Square	1385 Broadway
London	New York
WC1B 3DP	NY 10018
UK	USA

www.bloomsbury.com

BLOOMSBURY and the Diana logo are trademarks of Bloomsbury Publishing Plc

First published in 2007 by Gerald Duckworth & Co. Ltd
Reprinted by Bristol Classical Press 2012
Reprinted by Bloomsbury Academic 2013, 2014 (twice)

British Library Cataloguing-in-Publication Data
A catalogue record for this book is available from the British Library.

ISBN: PB: 978-1-8539-9701-3

Library of Congress Cataloging-in-Publication Data
A catalog record for this book is available from the Library of Congress.

Typeset by Richard Ashdowne
Printed and bound in Great Britain

The cover illustration is a detail from the Lyon tablet, now in the collection of the
Musée Gallo-Romain Lyon-Fourvière. The text is part of a speech that the emperor
Claudius, himself born in Lyon, delivered in AD 48 in which he argued before
the Roman senate that Gauls from north of the Alps should be given full Roman
citizenship. Tacitus gives his own version of the speech in Annals 11.24.
A booklet containing the authors' fair copies of all the exercises in
this volume can be obtained from www.lulu.com.

Contents

* These chapters are followed by one or two Further practice passages.

Acknowledgements

The authors are grateful to Clare Ashdowne, Marina Bazzani, Juan Coderch, Chris Collard, Richard Hitchman, David Langslow and John Penney. Our main debt is to Stephen Anderson and John Taylor who tested the material and made detailed comments on the draft. Their guidance has made this a much better book. We, of course, take full responsibility for any errors or miscalculations that remain.

Introduction

Unlike the student of a modern language who must learn to speak and write that language, the student who wants to learn an ancient language such as Latin never *has* to learn to produce a single word of the language but only has to read it.

What, then, is the justification for a book teaching students how to write Latin? We believe the answer to be twofold. First, practising the language in this way helps to fix constructions and vocabulary in the mind, so that a student can read texts with greater fluency, accuracy and therefore enjoyment. The second justification is that in the long term, by understanding better the challenges faced even by the ancient writers in composing elegantly in the formal version of their language, students can come to appreciate better the style, artistry and literary qualities of the ancient authors, at least in so far as they can be seen in the choices made in their writings. We hope that students will feel they have gained some of this appreciation by the time they reach the end of the book.

In writing this book, we have been obliged to make some choices ourselves. We have striven to avoid the excessively militaristic and political examples of old-fashioned Latin grammar books. Instead we aim to reflect the diversity of Roman and modern life in a way not done before in this kind of book: there are still some soldiers, politicians, emperors and slaves — they were a fundamental part of Roman life, and it would be wrong to neglect them entirely —, but there are also wayward boyfriends, querulous wives, and domestic, rustic and urban scenes. We hope these will prove as entertaining as they are challenging.

Richard Ashdowne   James Morwood
New College, Oxford   Wadham College, Oxford

About this book

This book is an introduction to writing in Latin. Anyone who has read undapted Latin texts will appreciate that different authors wrote in different ways, just as modern English writers do. It is also no surprise that poetry and prose often differ quite markedly from each other in both languages.

In this book, we introduce students to writing Classical Latin prose, the language of the most well-known and respected Latin prose authors of the first century BC. These authors include most notably Cicero and Julius Caesar, whose work was acknowledged in their own day as the embodiment of literary Latin prose. Both authors' use of language was widely imitated: indeed, it remained fixed as the model for Latin prose writing for centuries and it is the model that we adopt.

At the end of each chapter there are three sets of practice exercises, arranged in order of difficulty. Students and teachers should note that the C exercises are designed for use in revision and so should not be attempted until students have covered all the basic constructions. Between groups of chapters, however, we have also included short passages of connected prose covering the range of constructions met so far, and these can be used for both consolidation and revision as desired.

Every book about Latin grammar differs slightly from others in its presentation of constructions and use of terminology, particularly for more complex topics like conditionals. We have tried to make our explanations clear and accessible to students regardless of their previous experience.

One final note: at various points we have included lists of verbs that follow a particular construction. For the sake of clarity, we have indicated the conjugation of regular verbs with a number; the dagger symbol before a verb (e.g. †ueto) indicates that its principal parts are irregular and can be found in the tables on pp. 160–2.

Further reference

This book is designed to be self-contained in terms of syntax and vocabulary. However, we strongly recommend that students have a reference grammar such as Kennedy's *Revised Latin Primer* or Morwood's *Latin Grammar* readily to hand for accidence (the way in which words change their forms). Ideally, students using this book should also acquire the habit of making regular use of a good Latin dictionary, e.g. the *Oxford Latin Dictionary*, in order to check the precise meaning, forms and usage of Latin words, especially when tackling the longer passages.

Classical Latin was a literary language, related to but often less free than the every-day language of the Romans, which itself also changed over time. For the sake of clarity, an introduction to composition in Latin prose necessarily sacrifices some detail about variation in Latin in general. More advanced students wanting to find out more about particular constructions and their usage by other authors or in verse, should refer to B. Gildersleeve & G. Lodge's *Latin Grammar* (London, 1891) or to R. Kühner and C. Stegmann's *Ausführliche Grammatik der lateinischen Sprache* (2 vols, Hanover, 1955).

Use of the cases I

Nominative

The *nominative* is the case used for the subject of finite verbs (i.e. ones with personal endings):

> *The babies sleep.*
> **infantes dormiunt.**

> *The king loves his mother.*
> **rex matrem amat.**

> *The lions saw the horses.*
> **leones equos uiderunt.**

It is also the case used for the *complement* of verbs such as 'be' and 'become':

> *After the storm the river became deep, and there wasn't a bridge.*
> **post tempestatem flumen altum factum est, nec pons erat.**

Vocative

The *vocative* is the case used for direct forms of address:

> *Mark, don't trust that philosopher's words!*
> **noli credere, (o) Marce, uerbis istius philosophi.**

Accusative

The *accusative* is the case used for the direct object of verbs:

> *The king loves his mother.*
> **rex matrem amat.**

> *The lions saw the horses.*
> **leones equos uiderunt.**

1

Some verbs (of *teaching, asking, concealing* and *demanding*) can have two objects which are both in the accusative:

> *Why are you asking <u>me</u> <u>my opinion</u>?*
> **cur <u>me</u> <u>sententiam meam</u> rogas?**

It is used after the majority of prepositions (pp. 35–7):

> *The birds flew <u>across the lake</u>.*
> **aues <u>trans lacum</u> uolauerunt.**

It is used in exclamations about someone or something:

> *What a wasteland!*
> **o locum desertum!**

The accusative is used to express *extent* of time and distance (pp. 15, 18):

> *Ulysses was away from Penelope <u>for twenty years</u>.*
> **Vlixes <u>uiginti annos</u> a Penelope aberat.**

> *The senator advanced <u>five hundred paces</u> (i.e. half a mile) from his house.*
> **senator <u>quingentos passus</u> e uilla progressus est.**

With the four prepositions that can take either the accusative or the ablative (i.e. **in**, **super**, **sub** and **subter**), the accusative indicates movement:

> *The dog jumped <u>onto the table</u>.*
> **canis <u>in mensam</u> saluit.**

It is also used on its own (without a preposition) to indicate motion towards a place if that place is a town or a small island, i.e. an island named after its principal town:

> *I shall go <u>to Athens</u> tomorrow.*
> **cras <u>Athenas</u> ibo.**

This rule also applies to three very common nouns (**domus, -us** *f.* 'house, home', **rus, ruris** *n.* 'country(side)', and **humus, humi** *f.* 'ground'):

> *All travellers like to return home.*
> **omnibus peregrinis <u>domum</u> redire placet.**

Dative

The *dative* is the case used for the indirect object (i.e. someone or something affected by an action but not directly changed by it, typically a recipient or beneficiary):

> *I gave the boy food.*
> **cibum puero dedi.**

> *The merchant handed over the money to his daughters.*
> **mercator filiabus pecuniam tradidit.**

Although the dative usually expresses someone who benefits or derives an advantage from the action, it is used also for those who suffer some disadvantage from it too:

> *Three slaves stole the horses from the innkeeper.*
> **tres serui cauponi equos abstulerunt.**

Used with the verb **esse** the dative may express possession:

> *I have a ship.* (lit. *There is to me a ship.*)
> **est mihi nauis.**

The 'possessive' dative is used instead of genitives or **meus, tuus**, etc. with parts of the body, members of the family, and the like, regardless of the verb and particularly where contrast in possession is not emphasised:

> *The slave threw himself at my feet.*
> **seruus se mihi ad pedes iecit.**

Many verbs in Latin have their object in the dative case (i.e. an indirect object) even though their English equivalents might appear to suggest an accusative direct object:

> *At last we are approaching the city.*
> **tandem urbi appropinquamus.**

These verbs include:

†**confido**	trust
†**diffido**	lack confidence in
†**credo**	trust, believe
†**faueo**	favour

studeo [2]	be keen on, devote oneself to
placeo [2]	please
displiceo [2]	displease
pareo [2]	obey
†**nubo**	marry
†**consulo**	provide for
seruio [4]	serve
medeor [2]	heal
noceo [2]	harm
†**ignosco**	forgive
†**irascor**	become angry with
†**inuideo**	envy
†**parco**	spare
†**indulgeo**	be lenient to
appropinquo [1]	approach
†**occurro**	(go to) meet
†**succurro**	(go to) help
†**subuenio**	(go to) help
†**obsto**	stand in the way of
†**resisto**	resist
immineo [2]	threaten
supplico [1]	beg, pray to
impero [1]	order
†**praecipio**	resist
†**suadeo**	persuade

This list is a selection of the most important 'dative verbs' and they are worth learning.

Note that many simple intransitive verbs (i.e. ones which cannot take a direct object) have compounds with prepositional prefixes, and these compound verbs often take a dative:

There was a maidservant sitting next to <u>the old woman</u>.
ancilla <u>matronae</u> assidebat.

By the same principle, most compounds of **esse** (e.g. **adesse, superesse** but *not* **abesse**) also take a dative:

> *An architect was in charge of the craftsmen, but his wisdom did not benefit us.*
> **architectus fabris praeerat, sapientia tamen eius nobis non proderat.**

Some nouns in the dative are used 'predicatively' (i.e. like a complement, but invariably in the dative singular) with the verb **esse** to mean 'serve as':

> *The mountains which they found served as a great defence.*
> **montes quos inuenerunt magno praesidio fuerunt.**

We refer to these as 'predicative datives'. These expressions can contain a second dative expressing the beneficiary or person affected:

> *Knives are useful to cooks.*
> **cultri coquis usui sunt.**

> *My sister is a cause of concern to me.*
> **soror mea mihi curae est.**

Other uses of the dative:

- expressing the agent with gerundives, see pp. 112–13.

- with impersonal verbs, see pp. 76–7.

✐ Exercises

A

1 The women were very tired.
2 The freedmen are writing letters.
3 O what a sad poem, Catullus!
4 The soldiers handed over the prisoners to the guards.
5 The craftsmen had built a house for the king.
6 Many sailors sent their wives presents.
7 Cicero walked through the forum to the senate house.
8 My mother taught me philosophy, my father (taught me) the laws.
9 Your friend showed the priest the ring.
10 Nero grabbed the dagger from his mother.

B

1 The walls were ten feet high.
2 Servius was in charge of the ambush.
3 Clodia went to Pompeii, then to Corinth; finally she sailed to Egypt.
4 The cook had three tripods but no fire.
5 The teachers used to trust their students.
6 The citizens never obeyed the laws.
7 Wisdom benefits everyone.
8 Paula and Cornelia, go to the city and buy yourselves some jewellery.
9 Did you like the speeches, Mark?
10 The queen is eating bread and honey.

C

1 The children found me going into the kitchen.
2 Kings favour flattering citizens.
3 Old age proves to be the destruction of many.
4 The prisoners resisted the guards for a long time.
5 Shall we spare the leader? We have forgiven the other thieves.
6 Don't be angry with your son, but help him.
7 I know that your sister is very clever.
8 Having set out for Capua, Virgil stayed at a friend's house for three days.
9 I shall go to the country, where I have a farm.
10 It is said that Aulus lived 57 years.

Use of the cases II

Genitive

The *genitive* is used to convey meanings usually corresponding to English 'of'. It commonly expresses *possession*:

> the book *of the teacher*, the *teacher's* book
> liber magistri

> the *dog's* tail
> canis cauda

> the robes *of the priests*
> uestes sacerdotum

> the *farmer's* cart
> plaustrum agricolae

The genitive is also used to express the group or thing of which something is a part ('*partitive* genitive'):

> more *water* (lit. *more of water*)
> plus aquae

> enough *pleasure*
> satis uoluptatis

> many *of the senators* (≠ *many senators*)
> multi senatorum

Genitives usually express a connection between one noun and another. If the noun on which a genitive depends has a meaning related to a verb, the noun in the genitive may correspond to the 'doer'; we call this a *subjective* genitive, because it expresses what would have been the subject if the noun had been a verb:

> We were waiting for *the enemies'* attack.
>   (i.e. *The enemies* [subj.] *were going to attack.*)
> impetum hostium exspectabamus.

By contrast, the noun in the genitive may be what would have been the object, and this we call an *objective* genitive:

> *Paula could scarcely bear her longing for her husband.*
> (i.e. *Paula longed for her husband* [obj.].)
> **Paula mariti desiderium uix ferre poterat.**

These uses are very easy to identify from their context. Similar uses of the genitive are also found after some adjectives, mainly ones related to verbs:

> *The girl, wanting a new book, went to the market-place.*
> **puella noui libri cupida ad forum progressa est.**

> *Without meat people cannot dine well.*
> **carnis expertes bene cenare nequeunt.**

> *She gave birth to a daughter who is like her brother.*
> **filiam fratris similem peperit.**[1]

The genitive can express an abstract *quality* or description (although this is not usually something that you could see or touch):

> *He had a very devoted son.* (lit. *a son of great devotion*)
> **filius magnae pietatis ei erat.**

As well as its main use for connections with other nouns, the genitive is used with some verbs. Verbs of *accusing* and *convicting* commonly have either the *charge* or the *penalty* in the genitive:

> *The general condemned the traitors to death.* (lit. *convicted of a capital charge*)
> **proditores capitis damnauit legatus.**

The genitive of certain words expresses *value*:

> *I consider that poet of very little value.*
> **illum poetam minimi aestimo.**

With **esse** the genitive expresses a *characteristic*:

> *It is characteristic of an excellent cook to prepare food well.*
> **optimi coqui est cibum bene parare.**

---

[1] **similis** and **dissimilis** usually take the genitive, but the dative is sometimes found.

Other verbs that take the genitive have to be learned:

memini	remember (see p. 43)
†**obliuiscor**	forget
misereor [2]	pity, have mercy on

☑ The genitive is not normally used after prepositions *but* it is used with two common nouns used in the ablative singular like prepositions, namely **causa** and **gratia**, both meaning 'for the sake of, on account of'; these words usually *follow* the noun in the genitive:

I stayed in bed for the sake of my health.
in lecto manebam salutis gratia.

The merchants hurried to the port for reasons of business.
mercatores negotii causa ad portum festinauerunt.

Ablative

The *ablative* is the case used in expressions of the various circumstances surrounding an action. On its own, it expresses the (inanimate) *instrument* with which an action is done:

The girl was sewing with a needle and thread.
puella acu et filo suebat.

The cook cut the bread with a knife.
coquus panem cultro secuit.

The bread was cut with a knife.
panis cultro sectus est.

The ablative alone does *not* usually express the *agent* by whom something is done; this instead requires **a(b)** and the ablative:

The tables had been constructed by craftsmen.
mensae a fabris perfectae erant.

The *manner* of an action is often expressed with **cum** and the ablative:

The shepherd guarded the sheep with care.
pastor cum diligentia oues custodiebat.

9

However, **cum** may be omitted where the noun is described with an adjective or pronoun:

> *The widow embraced her children <u>with great kindness and grief</u>.*
> <u>**magna humanitate atque dolore**</u> **uidua liberos amplexa est.**

As well as these uses, the ablative is the case used after a limited number of other prepositions (the rest taking the accusative, see pp. 33–7):

a, ab	by, (away) from
cum	with, in the company of
de	down from, concerning
ex, e	out of
sine	without
absque	without
pro	in place of, instead of
prae	in the face of, in front of, ahead of
coram	openly, in the presence of
palam	openly, in the presence of
tenus	as far as

☑ It is well worth learning which prepositions take the ablative, since you will then know that all the others take the accusative. But beware **in, super, sub** and **subter** which may take either case; with these, the ablative indicates *stationary position*.

Some verbs in Latin take an ablative for what appears to be a direct object in English, often because of the instrumental force of the ablative:

†**utor**	use
†**abutor**	misuse
†**fruor**	enjoy
†**fungor**	carry out, perform
potior [4]	gain possession of [*also with acc. or gen.*]
uescor, sci	feed on
contentus, a, um	contented with
fretus, a, um	relying on
praeditus, a, um	endowed with
(in)dignus, a, um	(un)worthy of

10

The stone-mason was using <u>a chisel</u>.
lapicida <u>scalpro</u> utebatur.

Cicero is an orator worthy <u>of praise</u>.
Cicero orator <u>laude</u> dignus est.

Another instrumental use of the ablative is with verbs of *buying* and *selling* to indicate the *price* at which something is traded; this is usually a specific sum of money (contrast the genitive of value, above):

The freedman bought grain <u>at ten denarii</u>.
frumentum <u>decem denariis</u> emit libertus.

With events, the ablative alone may indicate the *time at which* and *within which* (pp. 14–15):

We arrived <u>on the fourth day</u>.
aduenimus <u>quarto die</u>.

An extension from this is the *ablative absolute* (pp. 21–3):

<u>As day was dawning</u> the bats returned to their belfry.
<u>die illucescente</u>, uespertiliones in turrim redierunt.

<u>After the people had been gathered together</u>, Romulus addressed his brother.
Romulus, <u>populo conuocato</u>, fratrem adlocutus est.

Note that the noun in the ablative here would not otherwise have appeared in the sentence and that this noun is the *subject* of the participle.

The verb **esse** has no present or past participle, and the ablative case is used alone:

<u>While Opimius was consul</u>, much excellent wine was produced.
<u>Opimio consule</u>, multum uinum optimum factum est.

As we saw above, the ablative is used with the prepositions that indicate *motion away from* a place (see also p. 17). Similarly the ablative may express *separation* more generally; other examples of separation include:

The jury acquitted the citizen <u>of the charge</u>. (lit. *<u>from the charge</u>*)
iudices ciuem <u>crimine</u> liberauerunt.

Related to this, some verbs and other phrases naturally take the ablative:

careo [2]	be without, lack
egeo [2]	be without, lack
opus est mihi	need
orbus, a, um	deprived of, bereft of

The guest needs money.
hospiti opus est pecunia.

☑ *Comparisons*

The use of the ablative to indicate separation is also found with comparatives to express the 'standard', i.e. the thing being compared with; this is the ablative of *comparison*:

The sailor is cleverer than the soldier.
nauta milite callidior est.

This method of expressing comparison is found only when the comparative adjective is nominative or accusative *and* the phrase which would become ablative is short; it is most common if there is a negative in the sentence:

Nothing is more attractive than virtue.
nihil est uirtute amabilius. (Cicero)

Otherwise, **quam** ('than') is used and the noun appears in the same case as the thing being compared:

The general favours soldiers, who are cleverer than sailors.
imperator fauet militibus qui callidiores quam nautae sunt.

✐ Exercises

A

1. Where did you find the athlete's discus?
2. In the end you flattered the emperor with sweet words.
3. Without light we were unable to see the children's faces.
4. Even a poor man always speaks with dignity.

5 But, (my) dear husband, I have never spoken to Julia's husband.
6 Plans have been drawn up by the shipwrights.
7 They know nothing about the architect's house.
8 The prisoners have been tied up with ropes by the guards.
9 The roof of the house was very high.
10 In the city, the herald walked out of the temple, across the bridge and
        into the amphitheatre.

B

1 A girl of great beauty was sleeping in the garden.
2 Why did you not notice the captive's flight?
3 The young man endowed with beauty approached Clodia with
        boldness.
4 Many of the Britons feared the Romans' attack.
5 The cook carried out his duty and left the kitchen.
6 The centurion's plans are cunning, for he is experienced in battle.
7 Don't misuse your power!
8 My bailiff is a man of great honesty.
9 Content with the old chariot, the young man bought a new horse.
10 The king's ambassadors went to great lengths for the sake of peace.

C

1 Men of this kind are hardly worthy of such a reputation.
2 Were you aware of his words? Surely you remember that story, or
        have you forgotten the old man entirely?
3 Pliny bought a country estate for a huge price.
4 Lions run faster than elephants but stags are the fastest of all animals.
5 A rich man is never in need of money nor lacking in friends.
6 The fugitive was charged with treason before the emperor.
7 A good writer typically writes delightful poetry; no one writes worse
        than a bad poet.
8 On the second day, the farmer had to hand over ten pounds of apples
        to the merchant, which the latter sold at a high price.
9 After the nurse grew angry, the baby began to cry.
10 When my statues were stolen, Decimus decided to investigate with
        me.

Time, place and space

Time

When

The time *when* something happens is expressed in Latin in the *ablative* case:

> *The pupils arrived at school <u>at the first hour</u>, and left <u>at the fifth</u>.*
> **discipuli ad ludum <u>prima hora</u> aduenerunt, <u>quinta</u> abierunt.**

> <u>*On the tenth day*</u> *Manius recovered.*
> **<u>decimo die</u> Manius e morbo conualuit.**

(The Roman day was divided into ten equal hours from sunrise to sunset.)

The following expressions also indicate *time when*:

now	**nunc**
then	**tum, tunc**
already	**iam**
still, even now	**etiam nunc**
not yet	**nondum**
no longer	**non iam**
once (upon a time)	**olim, quondam**
recently	**nuper**
at some future time	**olim**
meanwhile	**interim**
at length, in the end	**tandem, postremo, denique**
yesterday	**heri**
today	**hodie**
tomorrow	**cras**
on the day before	**pridie**
on the next day	**postridie**
at sunrise	**solis ortu**
at dawn	**prima luce**
in the morning	**mane**
at midday	**meridie**
in the evening	**uesperi, sub uesperum**

at sunset	**solis occasu**
at night	**nocte, noctu**
late at night	**multa nocte**

Note the *adverbs* **ante** ('earlier') and **post** ('later'), which can qualify expressions of 'time when', e.g. **paucis post diebus** 'a few days later'.[1]

How long

An extent of time ('how long') is expressed with the *accusative* case:

You searched <u>for seven hours</u> and found nothing.
<u>septem horas</u> quaerebatis nec quicquam inuenistis.

That young man is <u>twenty-two years</u> old. (lit. *has been born <u>for 22 years</u>*)
ille iuuenis <u>uiginti duos annos</u> natus est.

The following expressions also indicate *extent of time*:

for a long time	**diu**
throughout	**per** + *acc.*, e.g. **per totum diem**

The *adverb* **abhinc** ('ago') is usually accompanied by an accusative expressing extent of time, e.g. **abhinc decem annos** 'ten years ago', occasionally by an ablative of 'time when'.

During which

The time *within* or *during which* something happens is usually expressed with the ablative case:

The messenger will return <u>in four days</u>.
nuntius <u>quattuor diebus</u> redibit.

In this example, the messenger *may* take up to four days for the journey or *may* wait three days and return on the fourth; but in fact we are told about the time *when* the return will happen – at some point during a four day period – hence the ablative. Of course, if the journey really does last four days, the accusative could have been used to describe the same journey in a slightly different way; on the other hand, if the messenger waits before returning, we could have used **quarto die** ('on the fourth day') instead.

---

[1] Do not confuse this with the use of **post** and **ante** as prepositions with the accusative, e.g. **post cenam** 'after dinner'.

15

How often

Time *how often* is expressed with adverbs (see also pp. 156–7):

once	**semel**
twice	**bis**
three times	**ter**
every day	**cotidie**
again	**rursus**
for a/the second time	**iterum**
never	**numquam**
ever	**umquam**
sometimes	**aliquando, nonnumquam, interdum**
often	**saepe**
always	**semper**

Place

Where

Place *where* is expressed in Latin with the preposition **in** and the *ablative* case. But for the names of towns and those small islands which are named after their principal town, the *locative* case is used:

At Rome we used to sleep in a hotel.
Romae in caupona dormiebamus.

In Carthage, Dido was waiting in the palace.
Carthagini Dido in regia manebat.

Place names that are singular and in the first or second declension have a locative that is the same as their genitive; for all other place names it is the same as their dative. The nouns **rus**, **domus** and **humus** also have commonly used locatives:

Surely you don't live in the country?
num ruri habitas?

The slaves are at home sweeping up the grain lying on the ground.
serui domi frumentum uerrunt quod humi iacet.

16

From where

Place *from where* is expressed in Latin with the prepositions **a(b)**, **e(x)** or **de** and the *ablative* case. But for the towns, the islands and the three nouns mentioned above, the ablative is often used alone:

> *The chieftain walked <u>away from the general's tent</u> and went <u>out of the camp</u>.*
> **regulus <u>a praetorio</u> ambulauit et <u>e castris</u> discessit.**

> *When did you set out <u>from home</u>?*
> **quando <u>domo</u> profectae estis?**

Note that English 'leave' usually takes a direct object, for instance 'leave the city'. In Latin, words which mean 'leave, depart' (**abeo, exeo, discedo, excedo, egredior** etc.) almost all require an expression of place from which: the only common exception is **relinquo** ('leave behind') which does take the place left as a direct object:

> *Why did they leave <u>the temple</u>?*
> **cur <u>e templo</u> egressi sunt?**
> *but* **cur <u>templum</u> reliquerunt?** (*Why did they abandon <u>the temple</u>?*)

To where

Place *to which* is expressed in Latin with the preposition **in** ('into') or **ad** ('towards, in the direction of, (up) to') and the *accusative* case. But for the towns, islands and three nouns mentioned above, the accusative is used alone:

> *Then I ran <u>to the river</u>.*
> **tum <u>ad flumen</u> cucurri.**

> *Let's go <u>to the country</u>.*
> **<u>rus</u> eamus.**

notanda

1. 'the top of', 'the middle of', etc.: in Latin, these are expressed by adjectives related to place (**summus**, **medius**, etc.) agreeing with their nouns:

> *The old man walked to <u>the top of</u> the hill.*
> **senex in <u>summum</u> collem ambulauit.**

Although English uses 'of' here, Latin does not use a genitive.

2. If the name of a town or small island is used with a preposition, the meaning is often one of movement to or from the general area:

The soldiers came <u>to the neighbourhood of Capua</u>.
milites <u>ad Capuam</u> aduenerunt.

Other expressions of place

The following expressions also indicate *place*:

	at which	*to which*	*from which*
here	**hic** 'here'	**huc** 'to here'	**hinc** 'from here'
there	**illic**	**illuc**	**illinc**
there	**ibi**	**eo**	**inde**
the same place	**ibidem**	**eodem**	**indidem**
where	**ubi**	**quo**	**unde**
everywhere	**ubique**	**undique**	
somewhere	**alicubi**	**aliquo**	**alicunde**
nowhere	**nusquam**		
elsewhere	**alibi**		
inside	**intus**	**intro, intus**	
outside	**foris**	**foras**	

Space

Extents of place, i.e. space, distance or dimensions, are expressed in the same way as extents of time, with the *accusative* case:

They rode <u>half a mile</u> into the valley.
<u>quingentos passus</u> in uallem equitauerunt.

✐ Exercises

A

1. Yesterday we gladiators were already very tired before the show.
2. At midday the slaves stopped work because of the heat.
3. On my birthday at sunset my friends brought me presents.

4 The plague came in the eleventh year of the war.
5 Every day clients come to their patrons.
6 For six months the emperor favoured this sculptor.
7 Nine days ago you went riding late at night.
8 Once my parents used to eat meat every day in the evening.
9 Then they lost their farm; in the end they begged the gods for help.
10 Now they eat only bread and cheese during dinner.

B

1 In Rome, the law is greater than any man or god.
2 Lucius sailed to Alexandria and from there rode for three days seeking his friends.
3 On our way to Arpinum, we can rest at Titus' house for a few hours.
4 Everywhere I see decadence and corruption. Nowhere is there an honest politician.
5 In the fields foxes chased rabbits.
6 Leaving the bedroom, Livia went into the study.
7 Where did you see that poet before?
8 In the city, children ran towards us from every side; the citizens were rushing to and fro.
9 If we do not return in seven days, you must send messengers to Cato.
10 Nero was at Antium and refused to return to Rome for a long time.

C

1 Twice last year I visited my friends in Britain.
2 Finally, after several days, Spartacus was captured and punished.
3 Early one morning (just) as the sun was rising I heard a maiden singing in the valley below.
4 They had gone far away but you never forgot them.
5 The soldiers advanced thirteen miles from Rome and found swift ships.
6 Go inside, idiot, and tell the cook to come outside!
7 In Gaul, the inhabitants always resisted the Romans for a long time.
8 After sunset, thieves entered the building silently and stole my files.
9 In all his life, the merchant had never seen such riches.
10 The slave soon began to destroy books which Cicero had not yet read.

Participles

A participle is an adjective based on a verb; like all other adjectives it agrees in gender, number and case with the noun or pronoun it describes, but like its related verb it may have objects, adverbs etc. with it as appropriate. A Latin verb has at most three participles, which have different tenses and differ in voice.

Notice in the examples how often English uses other constructions ('while', 'after', '... and ...', etc.) where it is possible in Latin to use a participle.

Present participle

The present participle means 'X-ing'. It is always active in meaning, so the person or thing which it describes is the one doing the action. By 'present' we mean that it describes an action that is happening *at the same time as* the action of the main verb of the clause (which need not be present tense):

> *Did you see the boys <u>as they were running</u>?*
> **uidistisne pueros <u>currentes</u>?**

> <u>*As we walked in the garden*</u>, *we discussed philosophy.*
>   (lit. <u>*Walking in the garden*</u>, ...)
> **in horto ambulantes de philosophia disputabamus.**

notanda

1. The present participle is not used in Latin to make verb forms such as English 'he is singing', which is simply **canit** or **cantat**. But present participles *can* function like normal adjectives and have comparative and superlative forms:

> *No one is <u>more outstanding</u> than your boyfriend.*
> **nemo amico tuo <u>praestantior</u> est.**

20

2. When used as a noun, the Latin participle means *a person doing the action*, not the action itself (see pp. 109–10). Contrast:

(When he is) singing, he pleases me.
placet mihi <u>cantans</u>.

I like <u>singing</u>.
<u>cantare</u> mihi placet.

3. The usual abl. sg. ending of present participles is in **-i**, except when they are used as nouns or are used in the ablative absolute construction (see below) when the abl. sg. ending is **-e**.

Past (or **perfect**) participle

The perfect participle of active verbs is *passive* in meaning, and it literally means 'having been X-ed' or, more simply, 'X-ed'. The noun that it agrees with is the one that has undergone the action, and the action must have begun *and been completed* before the action of the main verb in the clause:

<u>After reading the letter</u>, you gave it to Mark.
    (lit. *You gave the '<u>having been read</u>' letter to Mark.*)
<u>litteras lectas</u> Marco dedisti.

We heard <u>the words spoken by the soothsayer</u>.
<u>uerba ab haruspice dicta</u> audiuimus.

He was driven out of the city <u>with stones thrown by the people</u>.
ex urbe <u>lapidibus a populo iactis</u> expulsus est.

☑ The past participle is used with the auxiliary verb **esse** in Latin to make *perfect* passive verb forms: **expulsus est** means 'he *was/has been* driven out' *not* 'he *is* driven out' (= **expellitur**).

Ablative absolute

In all the examples that we have seen so far the participle has agreed with a noun or pronoun that is already in the sentence for some other reason (e.g. as subject, direct object etc.) or with the unexpressed subject of the verb.

21

Sitting in the garden, I read the book sent by you.
in horto sedens, librum a te missum legi.

In Latin, past and present participles can also be used to form phrases describing the circumstances of an event, even if their subject (the noun they agree with) has no other role in the sentence.

While the philosophers were talking, we went into the brothel.
philosophis loquentibus, in lupanar intrauimus.

Here **loquentibus** agrees with **philosophis**, which is not the subject or object of the main verb and is grammatically independent of the clause in which it sits: the technical term for this is 'absolute' (from Latin **absolutus** 'loosed, freed'). In phrases such as this, both noun and participle are put into the ablative case, as you can see happened in the sentence above.

While the cat was sleeping, the mice ate the cheese.
fele dormiente, mures caseum comederunt.

Remember that perfect participles which are passive describe nouns that are the *objects* of the actions described. Thus, active verbs in English have to be made passive in Latin. For example:

When I had done this, I went away.

Here, first the English must be changed to include a participle:

Having done this, I went away.

Then because **facio** is an active verb and its past participle is therefore passive, we must make the phrase passive:

This thing 'having been done', I went away.
hoc facto, abii.

Further examples:

After hearing these words, Lesbia laughed.
    (lit. *These words 'having been heard', ...*)
Lesbia his uerbis auditis risit.

Once the temple was built, the priests sacrificed a victim to the gods.
templo aedificato, sacerdotes uictimam deis sacrificauerunt.

☑ Remember that the verb **esse** has no past or present participle: phrases just go into the ablative (e.g. **Caesare duce** 'when Caesar was general, under Caesar's leadership', **M. Messalla et M. Pisone consulibus** '(in the year that) Marcus Messalla and Marcus Piso were consuls'). But note that some compounds of **esse** do have present participles which are commonly used in this construction, e.g. **matre absente** 'in my mother's absence'.

Deponent verbs and past participles

Active verbs have *passive* past participles, but the past participles of deponent and semi-deponent verbs are *active* in meaning, so the noun they agree with indicates the person doing the action:

> <u>*After obtaining the bread*</u>, *the slave went to the butcher's.*
> **panem <u>adeptus</u>, seruus ad macellum iuit.**

> <u>*After the dogs grew angry*</u>, *the crowd became quiet.*
> **<u>canibus iratis</u>, tacebat turba.**

The action of these participles need *not* be completed by the time of the main verb:

> *The carpenter, <u>using a saw</u>, cut down a tree.*
> **faber <u>serra usus</u> arborem cecidit.**

The present participle of deponent verbs is active in form and could indeed have been used in this example, but the perfect participle is more idiomatic.

Future participle

The future participle means 'about to X' or 'on the point of doing X' and is *active*; it refers to an action occurring after that the main verb in the clause:

> *The gladiators <u>who were about to die</u> greeted Caesar.*
> **gladiatores <u>morituri</u> Caesarem salutauerunt.**

Its most common use is with forms of **esse**:

> *Virgil was about to read his poem when a member of the audience laughed.*
> **Vergilius carmen suum lecturus erat cum auditor quidam risit.**

notanda

1. The future participle is rarely if ever used in Latin in the ablative absolute construction.

2. The fut. pple is sometimes used in Latin poetry to express purpose; in prose, this happens mainly in later writers, but it was used, though rarely, by Cicero (e.g. at *Verr.* 2.1.56 **P. Seruilius ... adest de te sententiam laturus** 'P. Servilius is here to give his opinion about you'), and more commonly by authors from Livy onwards.

3. The fut. pple forms part of the future *active* infinitive (fut. pple with **esse**), and it then always agrees with the subject of the infinitive.

Past participle (cont.)

Like some other adjectives (e.g. those of place, like **summus**, **medius**, etc.; see p. 17), the Latin past participle may express a meaning corresponding to a noun phrase with 'of' in English:

> *The workers got up, before the rising of the sun.*
> **operarii ante solem ortum surrexerunt.**

> *They were punished for a breach of the peace.*
> **puniti sunt ob pacem ruptam.**

———

✐ **Exercises**

A

  1 While working in the dining room, the maid found a wax tablet.
  2 The actor left the stage laughing.
  3 After writing the books, the poet sold them.
  4 Once the bees caught sight of the flower, they flew to it.
  5 Do you like cooked eggs?
  6 I set free the prisoners who were bound in chains.
  7 We no longer want the statue sculpted by a very skilled artist and broken by the spear thrown by the young man.

8 Mourning and weeping, the mother stood near the tomb of the man killed by the thunderbolt.
9 You were chasing a man who is very loving.
10 Beaten with whips, the slaves collapsed to the ground unconscious.

B

1 Born in Arpinum, when I was a young man I studied in Greece.
2 Throwing back his cloak, the senator revealed a sword.
3 After putting the money on the table, the merchant picked up the amphora.
4 The companions set out from Pisa and travelled for three days.
5 The fleet arrived at Corinth and the people came out to welcome the sailors.
6 While the governor was speaking, the oldest chieftains fell asleep.
7 Panic-stricken by the smoke, the citizens fled to the port.
8 Romulus was addressing the people when a storm arose and he disappeared from view.
9 This lion is hungry now that the food has been stolen from him.
10 Why did they not trust a man loved and honoured by so many citizens?

C

1 Tacitus said the ship was about to set sail.
2 In the end, we reached the house of our friend who was on the point of sending out a search party.
3 Didn't you know that my father was going to buy a horse?
4 Thinking that Manius would not come, the conspirators devised a plan to capture him.
5 After mocking the miracles, Sextus said that he would not trust the barbarians.
6 The shepherd roamed the hills alone with his flock, after of the death of his wife.
7 Are you sure, Tullia, that you are going to write to me every day while I am away?
8 Once the money is handed over, give the buyers the keys!
9 After the destruction of Pompeii, Pliny returned to Rome.
10 In Caesar's presence he promised he would administer the province diligently.

Relative clauses

The relative pronoun ('who, which, whom, that') is one of the few English words which can decline, i.e. can change its form according to its function in a sentence. But unfortunately this fact is of limited use when one is translating from English into Latin, since the word 'whom' (which tells you by its form that it is not the subject of a verb) is not used very often these days.

> *I like a woman who knows her own mind.*

In the English sentence above, the relative pronoun 'who' refers back to the noun 'woman': the noun is its *antecedent* (so called because it generally comes in front of it). 'Woman' is the object of the verb 'like' and in Latin it would therefore go into the accusative, but 'who' is the subject of the verb 'knows' in the relative clause and would therefore be nominative.

The rule is that the relative pronoun agrees in gender and number with its antecedent, but its case depends upon its function in the relative clause which it introduces.

> *This is the man <u>who</u> met my wife in Capua.*
> **is est uir <u>qui</u> uxori meae Capuae occurrit.**

> *She is a woman <u>who(m)</u> I love a lot.*
> **ea est femina <u>quam</u> ualde amo.**

> *Who is the boy <u>whose</u> book you took?*
> **quis est puer <u>cuius</u> librum cepisti?**

> *Wasn't that the girl you gave the book to?*
> **nonne illa puella fuit <u>cui</u> librum dedisti?**

Notice how in this last sentence the relative pronoun does not appear in English (though it could have). In Latin it *must* be put in.

> *Those are the soldiers <u>who</u> the king was killed <u>by</u>.*
> **isti sunt milites <u>a quibus</u> rex interfectus est.**

If you are translating from English into Latin, it is always possible to discover the case of the relative pronoun by recasting the English relative clause as a full sentence. Thus in the first sentence above you can change 'who met my wife in Capua' to 'he met my wife in Capua'. 'He' is the subject and so nominative, and therefore the relative pronoun goes into the nominative. In the second sentence you can change 'who(m) I love a lot' to 'I love her a lot'. 'Her' is the direct object and hence accusative; so the relative pronoun goes into the accusative.

In Latin and English the relative pronoun almost always begins its clause:

It is Cleopatra whose kingdom I am entering.
Cleopatra est cuius in regnum ineo.

A superlative or emphatic adjective or a number (also 'many', 'few', 'the only') which goes with the the antecedent in English is usually placed within the relative clause in Latin and it agrees with the relative pronoun.

He is the most beautiful boy I have ever seen.
is est puer quem pulcherrimum umquam uidi.

If Caesar comes with the strongest troops he has …
si ueniat Caesar cum copiis quas habet firmissimas … (Cicero)

As well as relative pronouns, there are some relative adverbs (expressing place and time) which follow exactly the same constructions. For instance:

Soon we came to the forum, where we found the banker.
mox ad forum aduenimus ubi argentarium inuenimus.

I was cooking in the kitchen, from where I carried the food into the dining room.
in culina coquebam, unde cibum in triclinium portaui.

-ever

The ending **-cumque** is added to a number of Latin words to convey the meaning '-ever', e.g. **qui-cumque** ('whoever'), **ubi-cumque** ('wherever'), **quando-cumque** ('whenever'), introducing Latin relative clauses:

I like whatever books Apuleius writes.
placent mihi libri quoscumque Apuleius scribit.

27

Correlatives

Note the following pairs of 'correlatives'. In each pair the second is a relative pronoun or adverb.

tantus ... quantus ...	as great as
talis ... qualis ...	of such a kind as
totiens ... quotiens ...	as often as
tot ... quot ...	as many as

My intelligence is not <u>as great</u> <u>as</u> it once was.
non <u>tanta</u> est sapientia mea <u>quanta</u> olim fuit.

I read <u>as many</u> books <u>as</u> he gave me.
<u>tot</u> libros legi <u>quot</u> mihi dedit.

Latin likes correlatives. English speakers can find them a bit difficult to handle in Latin since they seem to lead to duplication of meaning. For example, a literal translation of the second sentence would be:

I read <u>so many</u> books <u>as many as</u> he gave me.

Idiomatic English would probably result in 'I read all the books he gave me'. Practice at using correlatives should empty them of their terrors.

With comparative adjectives and adverbs, **quo ... eo ...** express 'the more ... the more ...', lit. 'by what amount (x), by that same amount (y)':

The harder the slave girl works, the more tired she becomes.
<u>quo</u> diligentius laborat ancilla, <u>eo</u> magis fessa fit.

Literally, this example means 'she (the slave girl) becomes more tired to the degree by which she works harder'. Here, **quo diligentius laborat ancilla** is a relative clause.

The 'connecting' relative

In connected Latin prose, where somebody, some people or something in a sentence refers back to someone, some people or something mentioned in the previous sentence, we often find a so-called 'connecting' relative pronoun instead of a form of **is, ea, id**. This is often translated into English as 'and he, and she, and it, and they' etc.:

> *We spared the captives, <u>and</u> on the next day <u>they</u> brought us gifts.*
> **captiuis pepercimus. <u>qui</u> postridie nobis dona tulerunt.**

Here, **qui ... tulerunt** is a separate sentence, *not* a relative clause. However, the relative pronoun itself works in the same way as in a relative clause, agreeing with its antecedent **captiuis** in gender and number but being in the nominative because it is the subject of **tulerunt**. Connecting relatives are common in Latin, and are worth bearing in mind as an option for translating 'and ...':

> *The children were playing, <u>and</u> you told <u>them</u> to stop.*
> **ludebant liberi. <u>quos</u> iussisti desinere.**

Note, however, that the connecting relative is *not* used for the subject of a second sentence when the subject is the same as that of the previous sentence.

Relative clauses with subjunctive verbs

The verb in a relative clause is generally in the indicative. If the verb is subjunctive, the meaning is one of either purpose, cause or result.

Purpose

The relative pronoun is often used in place of **ut** after verbs of *giving* and *sending* (verbs of motion). The construction is the same as for purpose clauses (pp. 86–7), with sequence of tenses being followed.

> *The general sent out scouts <u>to find out</u> where the enemy had placed their camp.*
> **imperator exploratores emisit <u>qui cognoscerent</u> quo in loco hostes castra posuissent.**

> *I will give my daughter <u>a book to read</u>.*
> **filiae <u>librum</u> dabo <u>quem legat</u>.**

Cause

A relative clause with a subjunctive verb sometimes expresses cause: often the word **quippe** will be put before the relative pronoun to make this clear.

> *The sailors easily reached the shore <u>because they were</u> strong.*
> **nautae facile ad litus peruenerunt <u>quippe qui</u> ualidi <u>essent</u>.**

Result

> *Atalanta is not <u>so fast as to beat</u> Meleager.*
> **Atalanta non est <u>tam celeris quae</u> Meleagrum <u>uincat</u>.**

Here, her speed is not so great that it achieves the result of her beating Meleager: **quae = ut ea**.) The construction is the same as for result clauses (pp. 96–7).

Note the following expressions:

There are people who …	**sunt qui** + subj.
He is the type of person who …	**is est qui** + subj.

> <u>*There are people who*</u> *do not like Horace's poems.*
> <u>**sunt qui**</u> **Horatii carmina non ament.**

> <u>*She was the sort of woman who*</u> *liked older men.*
> <u>**ea erat**</u> **quae seniores amaret.**

This use of the subjunctive is often called 'generic' (from Latin **genus, generis** 'type, kind') because it conveys the result of people being the types they are.

notanda

1. **dignus/indignus sum qui** + subj. is the best way to translate 'I deserve to …, I do not deserve to …':

> *Sophocles <u>deserved to win</u> the prize.*
> **Sophocles <u>dignus erat qui</u> palmam <u>acciperet</u>.**

The literal meaning is: 'Sophocles is worthy so that (as a result) he should win the prize.'

2. **quam qui** is generally used after a comparative in such sentences as

> *He is<u> too cowardly to endure</u> the battle.*
> <u>**ignauior**</u> **est <u>quam qui</u> pugnam <u>patiatur</u>.**

The literal meaning is: 'He is more cowardly than the sort of man who would endure a battle' *or* 'He is too cowardly for the result to be that he endures the battle.'

✎ Exercises

A

1 Rome is a city which I always try to avoid.
2 Those who follow Caesar hate Pompey.
3 Lesbia is the woman who Catullus loved.
4 Ovid was the man who Cynthia was loved by.
5 I fear the general whose army is so big.
6 The flowers which I picked yesterday are withering.
7 The girls I gave them to were not pleased.
8 The general praised the soldiers whose courage had been so great.
9 Ovid did not want to leave the city in which he had lived so long.
10 Lesbia rejected the presents which Catullus gave her.

B

1 Give me the best book you have written.
2 The buildings of Capua are as big as those of Rome (are).
3 This is the only comfort I have left.
4 That woman's courage is of a kind that I have always admired.
5 (There are) as many men as (there are) opinions.
6 My palace is not as big as Nero's was.
7 You are the prettiest girl I know.
8 Octavius despised the few troops which Antony still had.
9 I like all the poems you have sent me.
10 This is not the sort of book I like.

C

1 He is too stupid to trust his teacher.
2 The more I see you, the more I love you.
3 Are you the sort of person who likes pop music?
4 Clodius has a sister, and I really love her. [*Use connecting relative.*]
5 I left the city in which my husband lived. [*Do not use Latin* in.]
6 Cincinnatus' wife gave him a toga to put on.
7 The man who has committed such great crimes deserves to die.
8 There are some people who despise pop music.
9 I sent a messenger to Athens to tell you the news.
10 Caesar was not so foolish as to trust Cicero.

Further practice

Whenever you are translating into Latin, it is worth bearing in mind that there is no need to keep to the exact format of the English. It is perfectly allowable for you to recast the sentences in any way that preserves the meaning and leads to a result that sounds like genuine Latin. If it seems a good idea, you can combine sentences in a different way from the English. And, if you are stuck, you can probably re-phrase the English in ways that you are confident of being able to put into Latin.

Students tackling the continuous proses in this book should have a look at the section on Word order (pp. 123 ff.), studying at least the sections on Adjectives and nouns, and Verbs, before they start.

I

While Coriolanus was attacking Rome, (his) wife, bringing (their) two small sons, came to (his) camp in the night with (his) mother, a woman of great courage. When he had heard this, Coriolanus went from his tent with the utmost speed. (As) he (was) about to greet his mother, she, now very angry, spoke bitter words to him. At last, overcome with grief, Coriolanus changed his plan and went away from Rome at dawn.

II

Once Rome was in great danger. While the citizens were despairing because no one had been found[1] who could save the city, the senators decided to send messengers to Cincinnatus who had lived in the country across the Tiber for many years. They chose him because he was both brave and clever. The messengers who had been sent to him found him working in the fields. After they had said what[2] the senate hoped, Cincinnatus asked for a toga. When he had put it on, he went to the city and soon defeated the enemy. When this had been done and he had returned to his farm, he worked in the fields again.

1. 'no one having been found'
2. **id quod**

32

Prepositions

With the ablative

- **ab, a** 'by, from' [*always* **ab** *before a vowel*]

  The children were terrified by the wolf.
  liberi **a lupo** perterriti sunt.

  Rome is a long way from the Alps.
  Roma longe **ab Alpibus** abest.

- **ex, e** 'out of' [*always* **ex** *before a vowel*]

  One of the soldiers suddenly ran out of the camp.
  unus **e militibus** subito **e castris** cucurrit.

  After a number, **ex** + abl. is an alternative to a partitive genitive (p. 7).

- **de** 'down from, concerning'

  Come down from the roof and tell us about your sorrow.
  descende **de tecto** et omnia nobis **de dolore tuo** narra.

- **sine** 'without'

  Don't drink wine without water.
  noli uinum **sine aqua** bibere.

- **cum** 'with, in company with' [*placed* after *some pronouns*]

  The shepherd lived with his sheep on the hill.
  pastor **cum ouibus** in monte habitabat.

  My friends were eating with me in the tavern.
  amici **mecum** in taberna cenabant.

- **pro** 'for, before, instead of, in front of, for the benefit of'

  Cicero spoke before the praetor on my behalf.
  Cicero apud praetorem **pro me** locutus est.

- **in** 'in, on, among' (*often expressing stationary position*)

  Merchants sell their goods in the forum.
  mercatores merces in foro uendunt.

  Candidates made speeches on the rostra.
  candidati in rostris contionem habebant.

- **super** 'about, concerning' ['above' *only in verse*]

  I shall write about this matter.
  super hac re scribam.

- **sub** 'below, under, beneath' (*stationary*)

  Gold had previously been hidden under the stone.
  sub lapide aurum antea celatum erat.

- **prae** 'by reason of, ahead of, before' (*usually metaphorical, rarely of place*)

  No plea was heard above the noise. (lit. *by reason of the noise*)
  prae clamore nulla adhortatio audita est. (Livy)

- **coram** 'in the presence of', **palam** 'in the sight of'

  Boudicca vowed in the presence of the women to attack the Romans.
  Boudicca coram feminis uouit se Romanos oppugnaturam esse.

- **subter** 'underneath'

  No one hides his light underneath a bushel.
  nemo subter medimno celat lucernam.

- **tenus** 'as far as' [*always following its noun, also very often with the genitive*]

  The young men rode as far as Brindisi.
  iuuenes Brundisii tenus equitauerunt.

  We rode with them as far as Bari.
  nos cum eis Bario tenus equitauimus.

- **absque** 'without' [*rare*]

  Without a plan, the runaways were unable to remain free for long.
  fugitiui absque consilio non poterant diu liberi manere.

With the accusative

- **ad** 'to, towards, for the purpose of' (*compare the use of the dative, pp. 3–5*)

  In the end the sailors swam to the shore.
  tandem nautae **ad litus** natauerunt.

- **inter** 'between, among, during'

  We sat down among the trees.
  inter arbores consedimus.

- **trans** 'across'

  The island you can see across the sea is Ireland.
  insula quam **trans mare** uidere potes Hibernia est.

- **per** 'through, by means of'

  Pliny made his way through the darkness.
  Plinius **per tenebras** progressus est.

  Through work and fine oratory that young man became consul.
  ille iuuenis **per laborem et eloqentiam optimam** factus est consul.

- **prope** 'near'

  Near the temple they found a well.
  fontem **prope templum** inuenerunt.

- **ante** 'before', **post** 'after, behind'

  Before the show, my wife and I had lunch.
  ego et uxor **ante spectaculum** prandimus.

- **apud** 'at the house of, near; in the works of'

  There was a poetry recitation at Servius' house.
  recitatio fuit **apud Seruium.**

  We learn a lot about courage in Homer's work.
  apud Homerum multa de uirtute discimus

- **in** 'into, to, towards, against' (*often indicating movement*)

  The cat jumped onto the table.
  feles **in mensam** saluit.

The Aedui made an attack against the Romans.
Aedui impetum <u>in Romanos</u> fecerunt.

- **super** 'over, above' (*movement*)

  The birds flew <u>over the trees</u>.
  aues <u>super arbores</u> uolauerunt.

- **intra** 'within', **extra** 'outside'

  The citizens were preparing arms <u>within the walls</u>.
  ciues <u>intra muros</u> arma parabant.

- **praeter** 'beside, past, along, beyond, except'

  The girls used to walk slowly <u>past the amphitheatre</u>.
  puellae lente <u>praeter amphitheatrum</u> ambulabant.

  I like all poetry, <u>except</u> Cicero's.
  omnia carmina mihi placent <u>praeter illa</u> Ciceronis.

- **iuxta** 'next to'

  <u>*Next to the cross*</u> *stood the sorrowful mother, weeping.*
  stabat mater dolorosa <u>iuxta crucem</u> lacrimosa.

- **contra** 'against, opposite'

  <u>*Opposite the theatre*</u> *are the baths.*
  <u>contra theatrum</u> sunt thermae.

- **secundum** 'in accordance with; along, after'

  <u>*In accordance with the Stoics' teaching*</u>*, we never despair for our lives.*
  nos <u>secundum praecepta Stoicorum</u> numquam de uita desperamus.

- **propter** 'on account of'

  He was reluctant to enter the cave <u>because of his fear</u>.
  <u>propter metum</u> noluit antrum intrare.

- **ob** 'on account of, against'

  He bought the farm <u>out of jealousy</u> towards his uncle.
  fundum <u>ob inuidiam</u> erga auunculum emit.

- **supra** 'above, over', **infra** 'beneath, below, under'

  There was sign above the door, on which was written 'beware of the dog'.
  titulus fuit <u>supra ianuam</u> in quo scriptum est 'caue canem'.

  Wise men consider all human things beneath them.
  sapientes omnia humana <u>infra se</u> ducunt.

- **sub** 'to beneath, to the foot of' (*movement*)

  Soon they came <u>to the foot of the hill</u>.
  mox <u>sub collem</u> aduenerunt.

- **aduersus** 'against, opposite, towards'

  The farmer left the cart <u>opposite the new well</u>.
  agricola plaustrum <u>aduersus fontem nouum</u> reliquit.

- **cis, citra** 'on this side of', **ultra** 'beyond'

  <u>*Beyond the ditch*</u> *stood a high wall.*
  <u>ultra fossam</u> erat murus altus.

- **circum, circa** 'round, gathered round, in the vicinity of, about'

  The forum is full; the temples <u>in the neighbourhood of the forum</u> are full.
  plenum est forum, plena templa <u>circum forum</u>. (Cicero)

- **erga** 'towards' (*rarely of place, usually of feelings towards a person*)

  Surely you don't feel hatred <u>towards your brother</u>?
  num odium <u>erga fratrem</u> habes?

- **clam** 'in secret from, unknown to' [*also + acc. or as adverb without a noun*]

  My friends brought my wife many gifts on her birthday <u>without my knowledge</u>.
  amici <u>clam me</u> uxori plurima dona die natali attulerunt.

- **penes** 'in the power of, in the keeping of'

  The republic is <u>in the power of the emperor alone</u>.
  res publica <u>penes principem solum</u> est.

- **subter** 'to underneath, along the underside of'

  The officer led the troops <u>along the base of the mountains</u>.
  legatus <u>subter montes</u> copias duxit.

37

gratia / causa

The two nouns **gratia** and **causa** ('for the sake of') in the ablative singular are used like prepositions. They take nouns in the genitive case, and unlike other prepositions they follow them:[1]

> *For friendship's sake, bring me back some wine when you return from the country.*
> **amicitiae causa fer mihi aliquid uini ubi rure redieris.**

☑ Most prepositions have a very wide range of uses and shades of meaning depending on the context: they may often appear to overlap in these. It is always a good idea to look up the preposition you are thinking of using in a Latin dictionary to check whether it is appropriate for what you are trying to translate.

Remember too that Latin has a lot of verbs with prepositional prefixes already attached to them (e.g. **exeo** 'go out', **praetermitto** 'allow to go past, neglect' etc.). Some of these compound verbs may still have a prepositional phrase after them (often, though not always, with the same preposition):

> *The soothsayer arrived at the temple.*
> **haruspex ad templum aduenit.**

Others simply take a noun phrase without a preposition (sometimes as a direct object in the accusative, sometimes in another case, very often the dative).

> *Regulus placed his homeland before expediency.*
> **Regulus patriam utilitati anteposuit.**

The entry for a verb in a Latin dictionary should help you to make the correct choice.

---

[1] We call them 'postpositions' (**post-positus** 'placed after') in contrast to prepositions (**prae-positus** 'placed before').

✐ Exercises

A

1 What do I know about peace?
2 The conspirators rushed across the forum.
3 Who threw an apple through the window?
4 Farmers often work in the fields before sunrise.
5 My girlfriend came to the villa with me.
6 Near the baths lived an old man by the name of Faustus.
7 Why did you go out of the theatre into the street?
8 Behind the stable the poor man found a chariot which was without any wheels.
9 On top of the Capitol is the great temple of Jupiter.
10 Loved by the gods, Aeneas fled from Troy to Italy after the war.

B

1 The people of Pompeii used to compete against the local villages.
2 Adjacent to the first arch of the aqueduct they built a small shrine.
3 After the lion was given food by a slave outside the amphitheatre, everyone except the condemned man was unhappy.
4 For the whole day the children played in front of the tombs.
5 Will you go to Antium instead of my father, who has to stay at Philip's house at Cumae?
6 There is always something new from Africa.
7 Even the best sailor is in danger when sailing between Scylla and Charybdis.
8 For so much effort they received very little reward from the foreman.
9 Because of this injustice you will pay the penalty.
10 Lucretius was not content with this fortune but wanted his work (written) about the nature of things to be read by many people.

C

1 Across (the whole of) Italy, people rejoiced at the good news about the war (waged) against the Gauls.
2 By the gate was a small urn under which, unknown to her husband, Rufilla left notes for her lover.
3 With a smile, the girl picked up the jewels.

4 Under the water we could see three of the sailors who had fallen overboard.
5 The consul spoke before the senate against the traitors arrested at his command.
6 I read in Cicero that wisdom is the greatest quality of human beings.
7 The family decided to wait for summer on this side of the lake.
8 The refugees had sailed to Carthage before disaster struck.
9 The senate awarded the *ornamenta praetoriana* to this man for his faith and devotion towards his patrons.
10 The other fields were beyond the nearest bridge at a distance of six miles.

Use of tenses

'Tense' (from Latin **tempus** 'time' via French) refers to *when* the action of a verb happened relative to some other time (either the moment of speaking or the time of some other action). Though similar, Latin does not have exactly the same set of tenses as modern English does, nor are they all used in quite the same way. In Latin, the system of tenses is also different depending on whether the verb is in the indicative or subjunctive mood, or in other forms (infinitives and participles).

Indicative

In the indicative the tense of a verb reflects when the action happened *relative to the time of speaking*. So the *present* is used for action at the time of speaking:

> *I open the door.* OR *I am opening the door.*
> **ianuam aperio.**

Notice how, in the present, Latin does not distinguish between single and ongoing actions.

In the past tenses, referring to things happening *before* the time of speaking, Latin does make this distinction: the *imperfect* expresses ongoing or repeated actions or states of affairs, usually ones which are no longer continuing:

> *You were carrying lamps.*
> **lucernas ferebatis.**

> *My father kept on causing trouble.*
> **pater negotium serebat.**

Because the imperfect has this meaning, it is used for background information, describing the circumstances surrounding some main event.

The imperfect sometimes has a sense of beginning (so-called 'inceptive' imperfect) or attempting ('conative') an action, or of the action being habitual:

The women <u>began to talk</u> among themselves.
mulieres inter se <u>loquebantur</u>.

<u>We were trying to build</u> a stable.
<u>aedificabamus</u> stabulum.

<u>You</u> always <u>used to steal</u> money. OR *<u>You were</u> forever <u>stealing</u> money.*
pecuniam semper <u>auferebas</u>.

The *perfect* expresses single actions, or states of affairs viewed as complete or completed:

Cicero <u>wrote</u> many letters. OR *Cicero <u>has written</u> many letters.*
multas litteras <u>scripsit</u> Cicero.

The boys <u>caught sight of</u> the girls. OR *The boys <u>have caught sight of</u> the girls.*
pueri puellas <u>conspexerunt</u>.

His uncle <u>was</u> notorious. (i.e. *was but no longer is*)
auunculus famosus <u>fuit</u>.

The *pluperfect* tense is used for actions that were already completed by the time that some other event took place:

They were grateful but <u>they had read</u> the book the previous year.
gratias agebant sed librum superiore anno <u>legerant</u>.

The *future* tense is used for talking about actions after the time of speaking:

<u>Will you send</u> me a letter tomorrow?
litterasne ad me cras <u>mittes</u>?

The *future perfect* is used principally in time and conditional clauses where the verb in the main clause is in the future tense or is an imperative: it denotes an action that will take place in the future but before the future action of the main clause verb:

After you <u>find</u> a good architect, you will be able to build a house.
postquam architectum bonum <u>inueneris</u>, uillam aedificare poteris.

> *If he <u>arrives</u> before sunset, he will please the girl.*
> **si ante solis occasum <u>aduenerit</u>, puellae placebit.**

Notice how, in English, the corresponding verb will very often be in the present tense, but in Latin it must be future perfect.

☑ Note also:

1. The emphatic forms of English 'I *did* do it', 'I *do* care' etc. do not have separate forms in Latin but they can be conveyed by putting the verb at the start of a clause; this is very common as an answer to a question:

> *Surely she didn't say that? Yes, <u>she did</u> (say that).*
> **num hoc dixit? <u>dixit</u> (hoc).**

2. Latin has no direct equivalent of the English 'have been doing' and 'had been doing'. If the action is or was still going on, Latin uses an appropriate adverb or adverbial phrase and the present or imperfect respectively instead:

> <u>*They have been working*</u> *since dawn.*
> **<u>laborant</u> post solem ortum.**

3. Some verbs in Latin have only perfect-stem forms: some of these have 'present' meanings, others refer to the past:

coepi	I have begun
memini	I remember
noui	I (have come to) know

4. As in English, some verbs in Latin are followed by an infinitive (e.g. **uolo** 'want', **possum** 'be able', **debeo** 'must, have to'). The tense of these verbs is usually the same as in English (but see also p. 77):

> *The scribes <u>wanted</u> to rest but they <u>had to</u> work.*
> **scribae quiescere <u>uolebant</u> sed laborare <u>debebant</u>.**

Subjunctive

In Latin, the subjunctive mood is used mainly in subordinate clauses, i.e. clauses which depend on the main clause of the sentence (hence its name, which means 'joined underneath'). Its tense tells us when the action happened *relative to the action of the main clause.*

43

☑ The Subjunctive Mood

The various uses of the subjunctive in Latin will become increasingly clear as this book is studied. While the indicative deals with facts, the subjunctive generally communicates non-facts, e.g. possibilities and intentions.

While you cannot learn charts of the English subjunctive as you can for Latin (and Italian, French, etc.), it is worth remarking that something which is certainly not the indicative is regularly used in English. It often contains the words 'may, 'might', 'would', 'were to' 'should' and 'could':

If my girlfriend <u>were to</u> turn up, I <u>would</u> be thrilled.

In idiomatic modern English, the first clause of that sentence would almost certainly appear as

If my girlfriend <u>turned</u> up, …

Obviously 'turned' does not refer to the past here; instead it is one way that English uses to express possibility, something which would appear in the subjunctive in many languages (including Latin).

Look at the following examples (taken from the *Oxford English Grammar* of 1996):

Israel insists that it <u>remain</u> in charge on the borders …
… customers are demanding that financial services <u>be tailored</u> to their needs.
… you can teach him if need <u>be</u>.

Most English speakers will recognise these uses, although in the first two examples, some speakers would use 'remains' and 'are tailored' with the same meaning; for others, the meaning of the first example would change if 'remains' is used.

The following is taken from *The Daily Telegraph*, 3rd February 2007:

I can see it would be unfair for Mr Blair to be forced out of office if there <u>had been</u> no wrong doing, and if he <u>were</u> still at an early stage in his mission to bring Britain to its knees.

The subjunctive is not necessarily as alien a concept as you may think, but be careful, since Latin and English do not always overlap in these uses.

Latin has four tenses of the subjunctive: two (pluperfect and perfect) indicate things happening and completed before the action in the main clause, and two (imperfect and present) indicate those ongoing at the same time as it. The choice within each pair depends on the tense of the main verb, and it follows a rule known as *sequence of tenses*.

Basically, if the main verb itself refers to the past, the subjunctive in a subordinate clause can only be either pluperfect or imperfect. We call this *past* or *historic sequence* (sometimes also *secondary sequence*).

Something similar happens in some English subordinate clauses, although the change is in tense alone rather than tense and mood, and the tense change is not always the same as in Latin:

[*Where <u>are</u> the dogs?*] *I asked where <u>the dogs were</u>.*
[ubi <u>sunt</u> canes?]   **rogaui ubi canes <u>essent</u>.**

[*What <u>did you do?</u>*] *We asked what <u>you had done</u>.*
[quid <u>fecisti</u>?]   **rogauimus quid <u>fecisses</u>.**

The sailors ran to the port in order <u>to look for</u> their ship.
nautae ad portum cucurrerunt ut nauem <u>peterent</u>.

The subjunctive is used in these subordinate clauses because they are indirect questions (pp. 64–5) or a purpose clause (pp. 86–7).

The *present* and *perfect* subjunctives are used in *present sequence* (sometimes called *primary sequence*); this is when the tense of the main clause is present, future or future perfect. The perfect subjunctive is used for for things happening and completed before the action in the main clause, and the present subjunctive for those ongoing at the same time as it:

[*Where <u>are</u> the dogs?*] *I <u>ask</u> where <u>the dogs are</u>.*
[ubi <u>sunt</u> canes?]   **rogo ubi canes <u>sint</u>.**

[*What did you do?*] *We <u>will ask</u> what <u>you did</u>.*
[quid <u>fecisti</u>?]   **rogabimus quid <u>feceris</u>.**

The sailors are running to the port in order <u>to look for</u> their ship.
nautae ad portum currunt ut nauem <u>petant</u>.

The Latin perfect indicative **adueni** may sometimes be translated 'I arrived' and sometimes 'I have arrived' according to context. We describe the 'I have arrived' form as the 'perfect with "have"', and it conveys a present state deriving from a past action. A main verb in the perfect indicative is usually followed by *historic sequence* for subjunctive verbs, but if it is a perfect with 'have', the sequence will usually be *present* instead:

I came to Rome	*I have come* to Rome *(i.e. I am here now)*
so *I could denounce* Verres	so *I can denounce* Verres.
Romam adueni	**Romam adueni**
ut Verrem denuntiarem.	**ut Verrem denuntiem.**

As you can see, something similar may happen in English with perfect with 'have' forms.

Sequence of Tenses – Summary

Main Clause	Subjunctive	
	Completed	*Ongoing / Simultaneous*
present future future perfect perfect with 'have'	perfect	present
perfect imperfect pluperfect	pluperfect	imperfect

notanda

1. Imperatives and other direct commands are treated as present tense main clauses for the purpose of sequence.

2. Though most subordinate clauses with subjunctive verbs follow the rule of sequence, there are exceptions (notably result clauses, pp. 96–7).

✎ Exercises

A

1 The painter is painting Venus and her lover.
2 Which temple did the emperor visit?
3 I was riding in the fields and fell off my horse.
4 They were able to reach Pisa before dinner because of the fair weather.
5 I liked Milo: he could tell excellent stories.
6 You drove the governor out of town.
7 The girl who sings most sweetly will receive a prize.
8 The whole city was burning but Nero did nothing.
9 Julia and Clodia are watching the show in the theatre.
10 All roads lead to Rome.

B [Practice for sequence of tenses]

These sentences naturally involve using constructions introduced in later chapters, and may be left for revision.

1 The craftsman bought gold in order to make a ring.
2 I will teach the sailors about the winds so that they can sail safely.
3 Decimus had seen the philosophers in the marketplace before, and went there to listen to them.
4 Hispala is writing a letter to invite her friend to dinner.
5 The shepherd's house was so small that the twins could not live in it.
6 If you read this book, you will understand how you can write Latin better.
7 The dancers do not know where the actors performed in Britain.
8 We want to help you so that your health improves.
9 He had urged them to wait and not to run away, but they were afraid.
10 Gather wood in the forest so that we may have a fire.

C

1 Quintus wants to be as rich as his grandfather had been.
2 Once, that man could jump higher than any of us and would always receive the prize.
3 They did warn us and we did nothing.

4 I had locked the door so that no one could get in but they climbed over the walls to hear my poetry.
5 The master has found out where I hid the gold.
6 On the sixth day, while we were despairing for our lives, the helmsman sighted land.
7 Mark refuses to speak to the girl until she stops smiling at the centurion.
8 Tullia has bought so many clothes that she cannot carry them.
9 When you arrive in Britain, make sure you send me a present so that I know you are happy.
10 These priests have been praying in this temple for centuries.

Pronouns

All Latin nouns have a gender, and their number reflects what they refer to. Similarly, pronouns also have gender and number, which they take from the nouns they stand for. Both nouns and pronouns have case, and this is determined by the grammatical role they play in their clause. Pay close attention to the gender, number and case of the pronouns in all the examples below.

Personal pronouns

For the first and second persons, Latin, like English, has words for 'I, you, we, me, us' etc. However, unlike English, the use of these pronouns as *subjects* (in the nominative, **ego, tu, nos, uos**) is relatively uncommon; instead the ending of a verb makes its subject clear:

> *I healed the sick man.*
> **aegrum <u>sanaui</u>.**

Putting in a subject pronoun, usually as first word in a sentence, indicates emphasis or contrast that would be marked in another way in English, for instance by tone of voice:

> *<u>You</u> write poetry; <u>we</u> read it.*
> **<u>tu</u> carmina componis, <u>nos</u> legimus.**

> *<u>I was the one who</u> found the body.*
> **<u>ego</u> corpus inueni.**

When not in the nominative case, however, personal pronouns are perfectly common and they are used as needed.

Third person pronouns

For the third person, Latin differs from English in two important ways. First, there is no true nominative in Latin that simply means 'he, she, it, they' (see below for what **is, ea, id** really mean). Latin relies on verb endings and context to establish the subject; if there is nothing expressing a change in subject, each third person verb will usually be understood as having the same subject as the immediately previous one.

Second, there are two different words meaning 'him, her, it, them' etc. in all the cases other than the nominative, namely **se** and **eum, eam, id**: these two are *not* interchangeable. Put simply, **se** refers to the same person or thing as the subject of its own clause; **eum, eam, id** always refer to somebody else.

> *Quintus told a story about <u>himself</u>. Then Marcus talked about <u>him</u>.*
> **Quintus fabulam de <u>se</u> narrauit. tum Marcus de <u>eo</u> locutus est.**

notanda

1. You will often find that **se** corresponds to English forms in '-self', but beware because English is more flexible in its use of, e.g., 'her' and 'herself' than Latin is in its use of **eam** and **se**.

2. In subordinate clauses, **se** may follow its general rule and refer to the subject of its own clause. However, in all clauses of *indirect speech* (i.e. indirect statement, question, command), *purpose* and *fear*, **se** more usually refers to the subject of the verb introducing that clause (i.e. the person speaking, fearing or having a particular purpose):

> *They asked whether he was going to release <u>them</u>.*
> **rogauerunt num <u>se</u> liberaturus esset.**

This rule does *not* apply in result clauses (pp. 96–7).

In a subordinate clause, **eum** always refers to somebody other than the subject of that clause. In clauses of *indirect speech*, *purpose* and *fear* it cannot refer to the subject of the verb introducing that clause either.

> *The mother, who is washing <u>her</u>, thinks <u>she</u> is a beautiful baby.*
> **mater, quae <u>eam</u> lauat, putat <u>eam</u> pulchram infantem esse.**

Possessives

Personal possessives in Latin (**meus, tuus, noster, uester**) are adjectives and agree with the noun they qualify (i.e. the thing possessed):

> *<u>My</u> book is excellent.*
> **liber <u>meus</u> optimus est.**

50

suus (used when the possessor is the same as the subject of the clause) also obeys this rule:

Lesbia killed <u>her</u> sparrow.
Lesbia passerem <u>suum</u> interfecit.

Horace likes <u>his</u> own poetry.
Horatius <u>sua</u> carmina amat.

In the first example, even though the English has 'her', Latin uses **suum** in the masculine because it agrees with **passerem** which is masculine.

The possessive equivalent of **eum** is its *genitive* (**eius, eorum/earum/ eorum**). This is *not* an adjective but a pronoun ('of him, of them' etc.): it does *not* change according to the thing possessed.

But many intelligent people refuse to attend <u>his</u> recitations.
sed multi sapientes recitationibus <u>eius</u> adesse recusant.

Demonstratives

Demonstratives ('this', 'that') are used to point to things. Unlike standard English (which has two), Latin has three forms:

this (near me)	**hic**	'this'
that (near you)	**iste**	'that'
that (near neither)	**ille**	'yonder, yon'

They could be used on their own as pronouns or adjectivally with nouns.

<u>These</u> sheep are smaller than <u>those</u>.
<u>hae</u> oues minores sunt quam <u>illae</u>.

Note also the following special uses of these demonstratives:

hic	**iste**	**ille**
the latter ...		the former ...[1]
some (pl.)		others (pl.)
my client	your client	

☑ Because of its frequent use in lawcourts to refer to the opposing lawyer's client, **iste** often has a contemptuous overtone.

---

[1] The logic here is that **hic** is the nearer, i.e. the one more recently mentioned.

is, ea, id

Technically, **is, ea, id** is a demonstrative; this is why it is not used as an unemphatic nominative subject. It usually only appears in the nominative if it is the antecedent of a relative clause or in order to change the subject by referring back to someone or something that was *not* the subject of the previous clause.

> *The ones whom they loved helped them.*
> **ii quos amabant eos adiuuabant.**

> *Julius loved Calpurnia. She despised Cleopatra.*
> **Iulius Calpurniam amabat. ea Cleopatram contemnebat.**

is never accompanies adjectives, participles, phrases etc. to mean a group of a particular kind, but relative clauses can frequently stand for this, often with a form of **is** as the antecedent.

> *Terrified by the noise of those standing nearby, she hid behind a tree.*
> **adstantium clamore perterrita, se ante arborem celauit.**
> **clamore eorum qui adstabant perterrita, se ante arborem celauit.**

Some

(a) English 'some' has many meanings and uses. Note the following:

pauci	a few
aliquot (indecl.)	a few
nonnulli	more than one
complures	several, quite a few
aliquis[2]	someone (rather than no one)
quidam	someone (a particular one, a certain one)

---

[2] Many forms in Latin contain **quis** or **qui**, which usually decline regardless of whether they come at the start, middle or end of the word. Like the question words **quis** and **qui** themselves, these words usually have two basic forms, each declined slightly differently: one is mainly used in pronominal forms (**quis, qua** (but **quis** as question word), **quid**), the other in adjectival ones (**qui, quae, quod**). Except for the nom. sg. of **quis**, its neuter acc. sg. form **quid**, and the neuter nom./acc. pl. **qua** *or* **quae** (always **quae** as question word), all the other forms of both are the same as each other and the same as those of the relative pronoun **qui**.

It is important to distinguish **aliquis** and **quidam**:

> *I was born on <u>some</u> (particular) day, I will die <u>some</u> (unknown) day.*
> **<u>quodam</u> die natus, <u>aliquo</u> die moriar.**

(b) With mass or uncountable nouns, 'some X' is usually **aliquid** or **aliquantum** with a partitive genitive:

> *<u>Some horses</u> were running in the fields; they stopped and drank <u>some water</u>.*
> **<u>aliqui equi</u> in agris currebant; constiterunt et <u>aliquid aquae</u> biberunt.**

(c) Latin also has the form **nescioquis** used for someone or something portrayed as indefinable (often contemptuously so):

> *<u>Some salesman or other</u> came to the house to sell new doors.*
> **ad uillam uenit <u>nescioquis mercator</u> ut nouas ianuas uenderet.**

(d) Don't forget the idiom **sunt qui** (**erant qui** etc.) introducing a relative clause with a subjunctive verb (p. 30):

> *<u>Some</u> people read his books. (lit. <u>There were people who</u> read his books.)*
> **<u>erant qui</u> libros eius legerent.**

Others

English 'some … others …' is translated into Latin as either **hi … illi …** or, more often, **alii … alii …**

> *The Romans conquered <u>some</u>, with <u>others</u> they concluded treaties.*
> **<u>alios</u> Romani uicerunt, cum <u>aliis</u> foedera fecerunt.**

Where *two individuals* are being talked about, Latin used the singular **alter** ('(the) one', 'the other') for each, instead of **alii**.

> *<u>One</u> works hard, <u>the other</u> is lazy.*
> **<u>alter</u> diligenter laborat, <u>alter</u> ignauus est.**

'The others', meaning 'the rest', is usually either **ceteri** ('ones other than those already mentioned') or **reliqui** ('the ones remaining, the ones left'):

> *The net-fighters refused to fight, but <u>the others</u> went into the arena.*
> **retiarii pugnare recusabant; <u>ceteri</u> autem arenam intrauerunt.**

Although two prisoners had escaped, <u>the others</u> were still in the prison.
quamquam duo captiui fugerant, <u>reliqui</u> in carcere manebant.

Different

Notice that where English uses the word 'different', Latin often uses forms of **alius** twice in the same sentence, doubling the meaning:

<u>Different people</u> did <u>different things</u>.
   (i.e. *Some people did some things, others did others.*)
<u>alii</u> <u>alia</u> fecerunt.

Same

The Latin for 'the same' is **idem, eadem, idem.**

She is <u>the same woman</u> as I saw yesterday in the marketplace.
<u>eadem</u> est quam heri in foro uidi.

Here, a relative clause follows **idem. idem ac/atque** can also be used:

We did <u>the same things</u> today <u>as</u> yesterday.
<u>eadem</u> hodie fecimus <u>ac</u> heri.

Self

Latin **ipse** corresponds to the English *emphatic* or *intensive* pronouns 'myself', 'yourself', 'himself' etc. It may also translate 'very'.

The master <u>himself</u> ordered us.
dominus <u>ipse</u> nobis imperauit.

I <u>myself</u> have seen the pyramids.
pyramides <u>ipse</u> uidi.

Agrippina fled on that <u>very</u> day.
Agrippina illo <u>ipso</u> die effugit.

With possessives **ipse** appears in the genitive:

Verres was condemned with <u>his own</u> words.
Verres <u>suis ipsius</u> uerbis condemnatus est.

54

Any

Just as Latin has several words corresponding to English 'some', so too it has more than one way of expressing 'any':

(a) In a clause containing no negatives, Latin uses either **quilibet** or **quiuis**.

> *You may say <u>anything</u> (<u>you like</u>).*
> **licet tibi <u>quodlibet</u> dicere.**

(b) Where a clause contains a negative (including verbs with a negative meaning like **nego** and 'virtual negative' adverbs such as **uix**), the pronoun **quisquam** or the corresponding adjectival form **ullus** is used.[3]

> *Everyone saw me and no one greeted me.* (lit. *... and not <u>anyone</u> ...*)
> **omnes me uiderunt nec <u>quisquam</u> me salutauit.**

The same rule applies after comparatives:

> *This student sleeps more than <u>any</u> of his fellows.*
> **hic discipulus magis dormit quam <u>quisquam</u> aequalium.**

(c) In any clause beginning with **si**, **nisi**, **num** or **ne**, the form used for 'anyone, anything, any' is the pronoun **quis** or the adjective **qui**, and they normally immediately follow that word.[3]

> *Is there <u>anyone</u> you are afraid of? (You're not afraid of <u>anyone</u>, are you?)*
> **num <u>quem</u> times?**

Each, every

The Latin pronoun for 'each, every' is **quisque, quaeque, quidque**; it almost always appears in the singular. Used with adjectives, especially superlatives and ordinals, it can often translate an English plural ('every single person (individually)' may be a more emphatic equivalent to 'all the people').

> *What <u>everyone</u> sees frequently is of little surprise.* (lit. *... he does not wonder at*)
> **quod <u>quisque</u> saepe uidet non miratur.**

---

[3] Similarly, **umquam** ('at any time, ever') and **usquam** ('anywhere') are used after negatives and comparatives, and are replaced with **quando** and **ubi** after **si**, **nisi**, **num** and **ne**.

All good men consider it right to lay down their lives for their country.
optimus quisque decorum esse putat pro patria mori.

The Gauls killed every tenth man.
Galli **decimum quemque** occiderunt.

Combining a form of **quisque** and one of **se** or **suus** (normally next to each other) gives the meaning 'each … his/her/its own' or 'all … their own'.

Every sailor longs for *his home*. (*All sailors long for their own home.*)
nauta quisque **suam domum** desiderat.

Where only two individuals are being considered, Latin uses **uterque** (again in the singular) for 'each', treated separately. Latin **ambo** (plural) denotes 'both' of a pair, treated together.

Each woman did what was necessary. *Both* survived.
utraque quod decuit fecit. **ambae** superfuerunt.

Notice how the English for the first sentence could also have been 'both women did what was necessary', while Latin can describe them acting individually or together. **utraque** is singular because it refers to each individual: 'each ____ of two'.

Each other

The Latin for the reciprocal 'each other' is **inter nos, inter uos, inter se**.

The priests were fighting with each other.
sacerdotes **inter se** pugnabant.

✐ Exercises

A

1 You saw the chariots in the Circus Maximus.
2 The barbarians live in huts; we build houses.
3 That bridge is older than this statue.
4 Cicero wrote a letter to you with his own hand.

5 This girl has lost her cat.
6 I read your letter and his book; the former pleased me greatly, the latter not at all.
7 You were the ones who brought them presents.
8 They were washing themselves in our baths.
9 His slave sings well; mine can hardly dance.
10 Clodia was friendly. She even told me her name.

B

1 I once knew a philosopher who lived in Corinth.
2 Some ran to the port, others to the temples.
3 A few of the audience walked out angrily; the rest laughed and applauded.
4 Someone has told the emperor about our plot.
5 Different people like different things to eat: anything sweet pleases me.
6 Every good husband gives his wife whatever she needs.
7 Never did anyone deserve a prize more.
8 There were tall trees on both banks of the river.
9 Lesbia has read the first of the books that Catullus himself sent her, but she has not read the others yet.
10 One girl loved Manius, the other hated him.

C

1 Many children fear ghosts may harm them during the night.
2 You didn't see anything in the darkness, did you?
3 The guards said they had seen no one.
4 If anyone offends the gods, there will be plague and no birds will sing.
5 Mark then went to the villa himself so that the manager should give him the profits.
6 They told so many lies that no one believed them any more.
7 Caesar told Ariovistus that he (Caesar) would not return the hostages to him (Ariovistus); Ariovistus replied to Caesar that he (Caesar) was a very cruel victor.
8 Each guest should bring his own servants.
9 Your client commanded the fleet not to attack the pirates nor hinder them in any way.
10 He will become consul unless someone prevents him.

Reported statements

English has two ways of reporting the words of someone speaking when they follow a verb of saying. They may be reported verbatim (**uerbatim** 'word-for-word'), in which case they are put in quotation marks; this we call direct speech. Alternatively they may be turned into a subordinate clause, often introduced with 'that'; this is indirect speech.

> *The woman said, 'I am very happy.'*   [direct speech]
> *The woman said that she was very happy.*   [indirect speech]

Latin has equivalents for both of these patterns.

Direct speech

Direct speech is not as common in Latin as in English, but its construction is very straightforward. It is almost always introduced with the verb **inquit** ('he, she, it says/said'), and the exact words originally spoken are retained, as in English. Note that **inquit** usually comes inside the direct speech, or after it, if it is very short.

> *The woman <u>said</u>, 'I am very happy.'*
> **mulier 'ualde' <u>inquit</u> 'contenta sum.'**

Indirect statement

The equivalent of English 'that …' after verbs of *saying, thinking, knowing, perceiving* etc. in Latin is the so-called *accusative and infinitive* construction. It is very common indeed. The *subject* of the verb in the statement being reported goes into the accusative case, and the verb becomes the infinitive.

> *The woman said <u>that she was very happy</u>.*
> **mulier dixit <u>se ualde contentam esse</u>.**

Literally, the indirect statement here means 'herself to be very happy'. English occasionally also can use an infinitive construction in similar circumstances, e.g. 'The woman considers <u>herself to be very happy</u>.'

Subjects in the accusative

Latin, unlike English, often does not express the subject of a finite verb if it would be a pronoun: this is because the verb's endings are sufficient. In indirect statement, however, the verb is always an infinitive, and this cannot change its form to indicate the person of the subject. The subject must therefore always be expressed. In the example above, the subject was expressed with **se** because it was the same as that of the verb introducing the speech. Contrast this with the following example.

The woman said that she (i.e. another woman) was very happy.
mulier dixit eam ualde contentam esse.

In indirect speech, forms of **eum** etc. *never* refer back to a third-person subject of the verb of saying, for which **se** and its forms must always be used (pp. 50–1). Notice also how things which have to agree with the subject must accordingly also adopt the accusative case (e.g. here **contentam**).

Tense of the infinitive

So far as is possible Latin uses the infinitive of the *tense of the words originally spoken* regardless of the tense of the verb of saying etc. This is sometimes difficult for English speakers to master, because English uses a rule of sequence of tenses for indirect statement.

However, Latin has only three infinitives (past, present and future) but six indicative tenses. The basic rule is that the past ('perfect') infinitive is used for anything that would have been in a past tense in the direct speech (i.e. perfect, imperfect, pluperfect), the present is used for reporting present tense verbs, and the future infinitive for future (and future perfect) verbs.

DIRECT SPEECH	INDIRECT SPEECH
I was writing a letter. **litteras scribebam.**	*He says/said that he was/had been writing a letter.* **dicit/dixit se litteras scripsisse.**
I am writing a letter **litteras scribo.**	*I say/said that I am/was writing a letter.* **dico/dixi me litteras scribere.**
I will write a letter. **litteras scribam.**	*You say/said that you will/would write a letter.* **dicis/dixisti te litteras scripturum esse.**

Future infinitives

(a) After verbs of *hoping* and *promising*, Latin very frequently uses a future infinitive in this construction where English might use a present infinitive alone.

> *I hope to send you a letter soon.* (lit. *I hope that I will send you a letter soon.*)
> **spero me mox litteras ad te missurum esse.**

A future infinitive is always found after verbs of *threatening* and *vowing*.

However, after **constituo** ('I decide') a present tense infinitive on its own is used, as in English, despite the future meaning:

> *Nero decides to kill his mother.* (*Nero decides that he will kill his mother.*)
> **Nero matrem suam necare constituit.**

(b) The future participle (and thus future infinitive) of some verbs does not exist, and the future passive infinitive (supine + **iri**) of most verbs is very rarely used. Instead Latin tends to use the phrase **fore ut** or **futurum esse ut** and a subjunctive verb (present or imperfect, according to sequence, pp. 45–6).

> *We promise the city will not be destroyed.*
> **pollicemur [urbem non deletum iri.]**
>   **fore ut urbs non deleatur.**

> *Everyone knew Caesar would be killed.*
> **omnes sciebant [Caesarem necatum iri.]**
>   **fore ut Caesar necaretur.**

☑ Because **deletum** and **necatum** are supines, they cannot change their form.

dico *and* nego

dico is a very common verb introducing indirect statement, but note that it cannot be immediately followed by a statement containing a negative. Instead Latin uses **nego** ('I say … not'):

> *The slaves said they did not see the dog chasing the cat.*
> **serui negauerunt se uidisse canem felem persequentem.**

This rule only applies to the first statement reported, after which negatives may be used freely and if **nego** was used, its negativity is ignored.

Remember that after **nego**, as after most other negatives, the words for 'any' etc. are **quisquam, quicquam, ullus** etc. (p. 55).

Why <u>did you say that no one</u> loves me? (lit. ... *say that not any one ...*)
cur <u>negauisti quemquam</u> me amare?

Cornelius <u>says that</u> Lesbia <u>never</u> visits him. (lit. ... *says that not ... ever ...*)
Cornelius <u>negat</u> Lesbiam <u>umquam</u> se uisitare.

notanda

1. English 'that' is very frequently omitted in indirect statement, as in the examples in (b) opposite.

2. Notice the differences between the following patterns in English:

Did you see the game <u>(that) Servius played last week?</u>   (relative clause)
Did you see <u>(that) Servius played last week?</u>   (ind. statement)

3. The accusative and infinitive construction is used for reporting main clauses that are *statements*. Reporting main clauses that are questions is dealt with on pp. 64–6, and those which are commands on pp. 69–71. Reporting subordinate clauses that are attached to any kind of main clause is covered on pp. 104–7.

Exercises

A

1 Then Sulpicia said, 'The children are playing in the garden.'
2 Then Sulpicia said that the children were playing in the garden.
3 The innkeeper says that the house is empty.
4 The dwarves said they were unable to climb the trees.
5 The senate heard the Romans had brought peace to Britain.
6 No one knows you found the hidden treasure.
7 Aeneas told Dido he had lost his wife in Troy.
8 The queen believed the hero would stay with her in Carthage.
9 Decimus' wife said she hated his sister.
10 This centurion says the city is being attacked by the enemy.

B

1 That old woman says we will one day be very famous.
2 In a dream the gladiator saw that he would be beaten the next day.
3 Everyone is amazed that so young a poet has written such a comedy.
4 Your sister saw that I drank only water.
5 All wise women know no one is prettier than Venus.
6 The merchant said he had not imported his togas and that they had been made in the city.
7 We discovered that Rufus was about to drink the poison.
8 Lepidina has promised to invite us to dinner again.
9 Julia said she had not been angry with her lover.
10 The cook told the master he needed a new knife.

C

1 From his youth, Cicero believed that he would become consul and save the republic.
2 When he arrives in Pompeii, Pliny will discover that many people have died.
3 As soon as Cicero heard Tiro was ill, he sent for a doctor.
4 The slave who had been punished with a flogging promised he would never try to run away again.
5 Some idiot thinks he can leave his chariot right outside my front door.
6 Every day during the drought slaves reported they had been unable to find any food.
7 Do you agree that flies are spreading the disease?
8 We used to believe Verres was performing his duties well; now we have learnt from the orator that that scoundrel deceived us.
9 Some said that the thief had been punished enough, others thought that he should do community service as well.
10 Ten days ago, messengers announced the end of the war in Gaul.

Questions

Direct questions

A. If a question begins with a question word in English, it will start with one of the question words from the following list in Latin. For example

How many days were you waiting?
quot dies manebas?

Where are you going to, my pretty maid?
quo uadis, o mea pulchra?

who? what?	**quis? quid?**
which? what? (*adj. of above*)	**qui, quae, quod?**
what sort of?	**qualis, qualis, quale?**
which (of two)?	**uter, utra, utrum?**[1]
how? (to what degree?)	**quam** (*with adj. or adv.*)**?**
how? (in what way?)	**quomodo? quemadmodum?**
how great? how big?	**quantus, quanta, quantum?**
how many?	**quot?** (*indeclinable*)
how often?	**quotie(n)s?**
for how long? (*of time*)	**quamdiu?**
why?	**cur? quare? quam ob rem? quid?**
when?	**quando?**
where?	**ubi? qua?**
where to? whither?	**quo?**
from where? whence?	**unde?**

B. If the English sentence is not begun by one of the words in the list above, work out which of the four categories below it falls into.

1. If the answer to the question could be 'yes' or 'no', you may add **-ne** to the first word (which should be emphatic) in the Latin. This is not

---

[1] Note that this word will normally be in the singular despite the idea of duality that it contains. 'Which of the two consuls do you hate?' goes into Latin as 'Which consul (of two) do you hate?', i.e. **utrum consulem odisti?**

essential. The question can be suggested by the word order, the sense or the context, as in English.

> *Are you going home?*
> **domum<u>ne</u> uadis?**

2. If the question expects the answer 'yes', the question will begin with **nonne** in Latin.

> *You are going home, aren't you? <u>Surely</u> you're going home?*
> **<u>nonne</u> domum uadis?**

3. If the question expects the answer 'no', the question will begin with **num** in Latin.

> *You aren't going home, are you? <u>Surely</u> you're <u>not</u> going home?*
> **<u>num</u> domum uadis?**

After **num**, use **quis, quid** to translate 'anyone, anything' (p. 55).

4. If the question is a double one, use **utrum ... an** or **-ne** (see 1) **... an**. Negative **utrum ... annon/necne**.

> *<u>Are you</u> going home <u>or</u> leaving Italy?*
> **<u>utrum</u> domum uadis <u>an</u> Italiam relinquis?**
> **domum<u>ne</u> uadis <u>an</u> Italiam relinquis?**

> *Are you going home <u>or not</u>?*
> **utrum domum uadis <u>annon</u>?**

☑ Note that in 1–3 above, it is the answer that the question *expects* that you are dealing with, not the answer that it actually gets. Thus 'surely he isn't dead?' is expressed in the expectation (or hope) that the answer will be 'no', but it could easily prove to be 'yes'.

Indirect questions

A verb in which the *voice*, *eyes*, *ears* or *mind* is used (for example, 'ask', 'point out', 'announce', 'perceive', 'understand') followed by a word which asks a question (see the list above) is followed in Latin by the appropriate question word and the *subjunctive*.

1. The question words are the same as for direct questions, except that 'whether ... or not' should be translated **utrum/-ne ... necne** (*not* **annon**). Also note **num** = 'whether' (regardless of whether the direct question expected the answer 'yes' or 'no').

2. 'If' introducing a reported question must be translated by **num** or **an** (=‘whether’), *not* **si**. Thus, 'he asked if I was ill' translates as **rogauit num aegrotarem**.

The tense of the subjunctive corresponds to the English, but sequence of tenses is naturally observed (pp. 45–6). Note that a reported past tense, whether imperfect or perfect, goes into the pluperfect subjunctive in historic sequence.

	Primary	Historic
Present	*He asks what I am doing.* quaerit quid agam.	*He asked what I was doing.* quaesiuit quid agerem.
Past	*He asks what I did.* quaerit quid egerim.	*He asked what I had done.* quaesiuit quid egissem.
Future	*He asks what I am going to do.* quaerit quid acturus sim.	*He asked what I was going to do.* quaesiuit quid acturus essem.

☑ Latin has no future subjunctive. For this construction we have to use a future participle together with the present or imperfect subjunctive of **esse** depending on sequence: see the examples in the bottom row of the table above.

Deliberative questions

Direct questions regularly have their verb in the indicative. However, the present subjunctive is used in questions that are *deliberative*, i.e. asking about what is to be done.

> *Am I to stay or go?*
> **utrum maneam an discedam?**

When deliberative questions are reported, the verbs remain subjunctive but their tense follows the rules of sequence.

Rhetorical questions

A rhetorical question is a statement made in the form of a question, i.e. it does not expect an answer:

> *What good man hesitates to speak for peace?*
> **quis bonus dubitat pro pace loqui?**

Here no answer is expected: the question is a rhetorical way of saying that in the circumstances *no* good man hesitates to speak for peace.

When reported, rhetorical questions are treated as statements and not questions; they therefore follow the accusative and infinitive construction (pp. 58–60), retaining their question word:

> *(He said) … What good man hesitated to speak for peace?*
> **(dixit) … quem bonum dubitare pro pace loqui?**

✎ Exercises

A

1 Why do you say horrible things about Clodia, Marcus?
2 You do love her, don't you, Catullus?
3 Surely you don't love such an immoral woman?
4 Do you prefer milk or honey?
5 How long will you wait for your boyfriend in the forum?
6 Do you like Horace's poems?
7 Which of the two boys do you like more?
8 Where did you come from? Where are you now? Where are you going to?
9 Surely it's me you're waiting for?
10 How often do you go to Clodia's villa?

B

1 I wondered whether my girlfriend would escape the notice of the matron.
2 He did not know whether his girlfriend had forgiven him or not.
3 I did not know whether my boyfriend would forgive me or not.

4 Did you know what your father was going to say?
5 I asked her where she was going.
6 He found out how long Cleopatra was going to be in Rome.
7 Did you hear what that naughty boy did last night?
8 I did not care if you made a mistake.
9 You told me why Antony had left you.
10 Did you discover why my girlfriend has left me?

C

1 Has Brutus left Rome or not?
2 Find out whether Brutus has left Rome or not.
3 How many children had Lady Macbeth?
4 Surely I haven't done anything bad?
5 How am I to know if my girlfriend is deceiving me?
6 I wondered what I had done to offend the teacher.
7 Do you know how many troops Pompey has led to Greece?
8 They wonder whether the gods exist or not.
9 Do you believe that the gods exist?
10 I have learnt what a good citizen ought to do.

Commands

Direct commands

(a) Second-person commands (i.e. commands addressed to 'you') are expressed in Latin by the imperative if they tell someone *to do* something:

> *Come here, friends.*
> **uenite huc, amici.**

> *Be present, faithful ones.*
> **adeste, fideles.**

Remember the irregular imperatives **dic**, **duc**, **fer** and **fac** from **facio**, **duco**, **fero** and **facio** respectively.

After a positive command, a second imperative can be added on with **et** if positive, and if negative with **nec** or **neque**:

> *Listen to me and don't go away.*
> **me audi nec abi.**

Negative second-person commands, telling someone *not to do* something are expressed by **noli** (singular) or **nolite** (plural), meaning 'be unwilling to', 'refuse to', followed by the *present infinitive*:

> *Don't do this, my son.*
> **noli hoc facere, mi fili.**

Alternatively, **ne** plus the *perfect subjunctive* can be used:

> *Don't say that.*
> **ne hoc dixeris.**

After a negative command, 'and don't' is **neu/neue**, but if the first clause is positive, use **neque**; both will be followed by the *perfect subjunctive*:

> *Don't insult me and don't praise my enemies.*
> **ne me uituperaueris neu hostes meos laudaueris.**

> *Praise me and don't insult my wife.*
> **me lauda neque uxorem meam uituperaueris.**

(b) First-person and third-person commands are expressed by the *present subjunctive*. The negative is **ne**; 'and not' is **neu/neue**.

Let him go, let him tarry.
eat, maneat!

Let's rejoice and not grieve.
gaudeamus neu lugeamus!

We call these subjunctives 'jussive', from **iubeo** ('I order').

(c) Note two useful ways of expressing mild or colloquial kinds of command:

> **fac ut** + *pres. subj.*   see to it that ..., be sure to ...
> **caue ne** + *pres. subj.*   take care that ... not

Make sure you come to see me. (Be sure to come to see me.)
fac ut me uisas.

Take care you don't fall. (Take care not to fall. Mind you don't fall.)
caue ne cadas.

(d) Note **utinam** with the subjunctive to express wishes; negative **utinam ne**. The present subjunctive expresses a wish for the future, the imperfect one for the present, and the pluperfect a wish that something had been the case in the past. The subjunctive can express these meanings on its own, but **utinam** is often used.

May you be happy!
(utinam) felix sis!

If only I were happy!
utinam felix essem!

If only I had not been absent!
utinam ne abfuissem!

Indirect *or* reported commands

(a) With two exceptions, all Latin words of *ordering* and *forbidding* (i.e. telling not to) are followed by **ut** or **ne** and the present or imperfect subjunctive (depending on sequence of tenses – see pp. 45–6); 'and not' is **neue** or **neu**.

> *Hadrian <u>ordered</u> his soldiers <u>to build</u> a wall.*
> **Hadrianus militibus <u>imperauit ut</u> murum <u>aedificarent</u>.**

> *Hadrian <u>told</u> his wife <u>not to come</u> with him to his villa.*
> **Hadrianus uxori <u>imperauit ne</u> ad uillam secum <u>iret</u>.**

Note that the word 'tell' is often used in English as a synonym for 'order'. Be careful to distinguish this use of 'tell' from those when it means 'inform', 'announce' or 'narrate'.

(b) Since English tends to use an infinitive after a verb of ordering ('I order you <u>to do</u> this') a common mistake is to follow suit in Latin. You must be very careful not to fall into this trap.

However, there are two verbs which introduce indirect commands that *are* followed by the accusative and infinitive.

iubeo, -ere, iussi, iussum	order
ueto, -are, uetui, uetitum	order … not, forbid

> *She <u>told</u> me <u>to avoid</u> her.*
> **me <u>iussit</u> se <u>uitare</u>.**

> *He <u>told</u> his wife <u>not to return</u> home.*
> **uxorem <u>uetuit</u> domum <u>redire</u>.**

Note that **iubeo** cannot be followed by **non** *except* where **non** negatives a single word. Otherwise **ueto** or **impero ne** must be used instead.

> *I order you to do <u>not this</u> but that.*
> **iubeo te <u>non hoc</u> agere sed illud.**

(c) Note that the indirect command construction does not only follow verbs of commanding or forbidding. It can follow any verb through which one is trying to persuade someone to do or not to do something, e.g. 'persuade', 'advise', 'beg', 'encourage', 'warn', 'ask', etc.

> *The Britains <u>desired</u> us to leave. We <u>begged</u> them not to send us away.*
> **Britanni <u>optauerunt</u> ut abiremus. <u>orauimus</u> eos ne nos dimitterent.**

Remember, however, that English 'ask' can also introduce indirect questions. So too can Latin **rogo**. Distinguish carefully between:

I asked Hercules to give me the apples.
Herculem rogaui ut mihi mala traderet.

I asked Hercules how many apples he was holding.
Herculem rogaui quot mala teneret.

Some verbs commonly used in this construction are followed by the dative:

impero [1]	order
mando [1]	order
†praecipio	order
†(per-)suadeo	urge, persuade

They persuaded me to help them.
<u>mihi persuaserunt</u> ut se adiuuarem.

✐ Exercises

A

1 Spin, mother, and I shall sew.
2 Follow your leader.
3 Don't throw stones, boys.
4 Eat your dinner and don't vomit, girls.
5 Don't drink too much, students, and don't play your music very loud.
6 Let's all go down to the river.
7 Let them eat cake!
8 Let's not delay.
9 (Please) make sure you come to my recitation.
10 Come to my party and don't take listen to the comments of old men.

B

1 I told the boys to work very hard.
2 I am trying to persuade the girls to stop their hard work.
3 Stephanus will urge the masters to admit girls into the school.

4 Antony encouraged the soldiers to follow Caesar.
5 The philosopher advised his pupils to study wisdom.
6 I am begging the gods to help me in my Latin studies.
7 I prayed that I might succeed in my exam.
8 We forbid you to work any longer.
9 My father told me to forgive my enemies.
10 I am asking you to help me.

C

1 Let's leave the city and not think about work!
2 I advised her to leave her boyfriend and not to see him again.
3 Do this! I warn you not to do that.
4 He prayed to the gods that he should beat the others in the race.
5 The girl told her mother to marry the old man.
6 Don't sleep when I am teaching. I advise you to stay awake in future.
7 They warned their friend to avoid Horace's recital. They should listen
    to Virgil's poems.
8 Apollo ordered Orestes to kill his mother and not to be afraid.
9 Kill your mother, Orestes, and don't be afraid.
10 Let Orestes kill his mother and not be afraid!

Further practice

III

An old woman came to King Tarquin and told him that she had brought nine books. She said that these were sacred oracles and asked the king if he wished to buy them. He asked her how much money she wanted; she told him to pay (give) her a huge price. The king refused and she burnt three books[1] and asked him whether he was going to buy the remaining six at the same price or not. Again he said that he would not buy them. When she had burnt three more[2] books,[1] he told her to sell him the remaining (ones). He paid the woman the same price as (which) she had asked for all of them.[3]

1. ablative absolute
2. **alius**
3. **pro** + abl.

IV

There was once a girl whose name was Psyche. Venus, who did not admire her beauty, called her son Cupid, whose arrows wound so many mortals, said that she was very angry, and told him to avenge his mother. 'What is happening?' she said. 'That[1] girl inflames all mortals with love. Who does not love her? What am I to do? Make her fall in love with[2] the most wretched man who lives on earth!' She asked him why he was delaying. Cupid was inflamed with anger. He loved his mother whom nobody now worshipped, and he knew what she wanted. Therefore he said he would obey her and quickly flew to the country where Psyche lived.

1. Venus is expressing contempt.
2. 'may she love'

Verbs

Transitive and intransitive verbs

The parents <u>drank</u> wine; the children <u>slept</u>.
uinum <u>biberunt</u> parentes; liberi <u>dormiebant</u>.

There are two basic types of verb in English and Latin. Some, like 'drink', can take a direct object (a thing directly acted on by the verb): these we call *transitive*. Others, like 'sleep', cannot take a direct object: these we call *intransitive*.

In English, many verbs can be either transitive or intransitive depending on whether the object is expressed or not, or even on what the verb's subject is:

The student was reading (a book). The birds were singing.

The pirates sank the ship. The ship sank.

In Latin, transitive verbs are those which have a direct object in the accusative case: verbs which take other cases (i.e. genitive, dative or ablative) or no case at all are *intransitive* in Latin even though their English equivalent may be transitive:

The parents <u>had dinner</u>.
parentes <u>cenauerunt</u>.

The children <u>obeyed</u> their teacher.
liberi magistro <u>paruerunt</u>.

Most Latin verbs are inherently transitive or intransitive: you can't just choose, as in English. As a general rule, if a Latin verb is transitive, it not only *can* have a direct object but *should* have one *unless* that object can be immediately understood from the context.

Should we eat <u>the apples</u> or throw <u>them</u> away? Throw <u>them</u> away!
edamusne <u>mala</u> an abiciamus (<u>...</u>) ? abicite (<u>...</u>) !

When writing Latin, it is vital to know if a Latin verb is transitive or not.

74

Passive verbs

By making a Latin verb passive, the direct object of an active verb becomes the subject of the passive verb, and the original agent is then omitted or, if it is kept, appears in the ablative after **a(b)**.

> *We help <u>the shipwrecked men</u>.   <u>The shipwrecked men</u> are helped by us.*
> **<u>naufragos</u> adiuuamus.   <u>naufragi</u> a nobis adiuuantur.**

It should be obvious therefore that only those verbs which have direct objects (i.e. transitive verbs) can have true passive forms. Latin *cannot* do what English does with 'Servius is offered a present by Tullia', where 'Servius' is *not* the direct object in the active sentence 'Tullia offers a present <u>to Servius</u>'.

Deponent verbs

Some Latin verbs always have a passive form but do not have a passive meaning. We call these 'deponent'. Many deponent verbs are intransitive, but some are transitive and so take direct objects exactly like normal active verbs.

> *I <u>embrace</u> my mother and <u>set out</u>.*
> **<u>amplector</u> matrem et <u>proficiscor</u>.**

Finite forms of transitive deponent verbs, i.e. ones that have person and number, *cannot* be used with passive meaning. Moreover, all the participles (including the past participle) and the gerund of deponent verbs are active in meaning; their only form with passive meaning is the gerundive (p. 112).

Latin has a small number of semi-deponent verbs (for instance **gaudeo, gaudere, gauisus sum** 'rejoice'), which are deponent only in the perfect, pluperfect and future perfect tenses.

Impersonal verbs

Verbs like 'sing', 'read', 'be ill' etc. have meanings involving someone, the subject, doing or being something. However, there are some verbs in both English and Latin which do not have a 'real' subject but instead have something filling in for where a subject ought to be. We describe these verbs as *impersonal*. In English, the stand-in subject is usually 'it', a neuter third-person singular pronoun. In Latin, there is no pronoun, just the third-person singular form of the verb.

Typical impersonal verbs include expressions of weather and time:

pluit	it is raining
ningit	it is snowing
fulgurat	there is lightning
tonat	there is thunder
lucescit	it is dawn
uesperascit	it grows late

Latin, however, also has a number of impersonal expressions that correspond to personal verbs in English. For instance, the following verbs express *feelings*:

me miseret	I pity
me paenitet	I regret
me piget	I am bored of
me pudet	I am ashamed of
me taedet	I am tired of

With all of these, the *person who feels* is in the *accusative* and the *source of the feeling* is in the *genitive* (or if an action, it may be an infinitive).

> *Plautus is bored of work. He regrets laughing.*
> **Plautum piget laboris. eum paenitet ridere.**

Note also the following which express things like *duty, obligation, permission* etc. and are usually followed by an infinitive; some of these verbs take a accusative of the person involved, others a dative:

me ire oportet	I have a duty to go, I should go
me ire decet	it is fitting for me to go
me ire dedecet	it is unfitting for me to go
me ire iuuat	I like going
mihi ire placet	I like going
mihi ire uidetur	I decide to go
mihi ire libet	I like going
mihi ire (per eum) licet	I am permitted (by him)
necesse est mihi ire	I must go

It was not fitting for Cato to laugh.
Catonem non <u>decebat</u> ridere.

I permit you to marry my daughter.
<u>per me</u> tibi <u>licet</u> filiam meam in matrimonium ducere.

Note that many of these verbs belong to the second conjugation. Impersonal verbs can appear in any tense of the indicative or subjunctive, and they have an infinitive for use in indirect speech (which appears without an accusative subject, since they have no subject).

Caeso said <u>he gave him permission</u> to marry his daughter.
Caeso dixit <u>per se licere</u> ei filiam suam in matrimonium ducere.

☑ Be careful with the tense of Latin **oportet** when translating English 'should' and 'ought to'. Where English has 'should have done' or 'ought to have done', Latin uses the past tense of **oportet** with a present infinitive, because the obligation was also in the past.

Cato <u>should</u> not <u>have</u> laughed. (Cato 'did not ought' to laugh.)
Catonem non <u>oportuit</u> ridere.

The passive of intransitive verbs

Only transitive verbs can have a true passive. However, intransitive verbs may appear in the passive in Latin, but when they do, they become impersonal (i.e. neuter third-person singular); any 'objects' that they may have had (always in cases other than the accusative) then *remain* in the same case.

We persuade the philosophers   *The philosophers <u>are persuaded</u> by us.*
philosophis persuademus.   **philosophis <u>persuadetur</u> a nobis.**

Here a literal translation would be 'we persuade to the philosophers' and 'it is persuaded to the philosophers by us'. This is why it is important to know whether a verb is transitive or intransitive in Latin: since **persuadeo** does not take the accusative, the only way to make a passive 'I am persuaded' is to use the verb impersonally and keep the person persuaded in the dative case.

Even intransitive verbs which take no case at all may be used impersonally if we do not want to specify the person doing them (e.g. because it is being done generally):

> *People are arriving at the city.* (lit. *There is arriving at the city.*)
> **ad urbem <u>aduenitur</u>.**

> *The battle was long and hard.* (lit. *It was fought* ...)
> **diu atque acriter pugnatum est.**

This general rule that intransitive verbs can only be used impersonally in the passive explains why they appear in the neuter singular when used as a gerundive (pp. 112–13).

☑ Verbs of *saying* etc. are rarely used impersonally in the passive in Latin, unlike in English. Latin prefers a personal passive with a *nominative* subject:

> *It is said that <u>Catullus</u> loved Lesbia.* (lit. *Catullus is said to have loved Lesbia.*)
> **<u>Catullus</u> dicitur Lesbiam amauisse.**
>   [NOT **dicitur <u>Catullum</u> Lesbiam amauisse.**]

✐ Exercises

A

  1 The prisoners are escaping from the prison.
  2 Open the door!
  3 Can you see Vesuvius?
  4 The emperor favours Epaphroditus.
  5 We are tired and we are hungry.
  6 The farmers are ploughing the fields and sowing the seed.
  7 Why did Mettius build that aqueduct?
  8 The sailors trust the gods.
  9 A freedman gave the dog a bone.
10 Women were hurrying to the marketplace.

B

  1 It is fitting for daughters to obey their fathers.
  2 Slaves are not permitted to wear togas.

3 Did you say it was raining?
4 Brutus is tired of speeches.
5 No one regrets the death of a tyrant.
6 Nero must take better care of his mother.
7 Country people like hunting.
8 As it was growing dark, it began to snow.
9 Surely Lesbia is not ashamed of her handsome lover?
10 A rich man took pity on that sad poor man.

C

1 You should have sent scouts to steal the statue.
2 The thieves captured during the night will not be pardoned.
3 Lions should never be trusted.
4 The Greeks were resisted by the Trojans for a long time.
5 As it grew light, people came from every side.
6 When you decided to stay, why were you not hindered by the others?
7 Valerius was thanked for bringing such a magnificent cake.
8 We have been ordered to seize your books.
9 My doctor said I must sleep.
10 Don't be persuaded by deceitful salesmen!

Time clauses

Time clauses are used to express *when* the action of some other clause took place. Words such as the following are used to introduce such clauses.

when[1]	**ubi, ut**
while	**quamdiu**
as often as	**quotiens**
as soon as	**simul atque/ac, ut primum, cum primum**
after	**post(ea)quam**
since	**ex quo (tempore)**

In Latin, the verb in time clauses introduced by these is normally in the indicative.

> *I left the forum after my friend <u>arrived</u>.*
> **e foro exii postquam amicus meus <u>aduenit</u>.**

> *Whenever cats <u>see</u> mice, they feel hungry.*
> **quotiens feles mures <u>uident</u>, esuriunt.**

notanda

1. The 'concealed' future in English:

> *After I <u>arrive</u>, I will give you the letter.*
> **postquam <u>aduenero</u>, litteras tibi dabo.**

At first sight the English seems to call for a present tense, but Latin needs the future perfect (*not* the future). The arrival will be in the *future* and the giving will happen *after* the arrival.

2. **postquam (posteaquam), ubi, ut, simul atque (simul ac), ut primum** and **cum primum** are all followed by the *perfect* indicative when they refer to past time. English is likely to use a pluperfect.

---

[1] Note that **quando** is a question word and is *not* used to introduce a time clause. Think carefully about 'she asked him when he had arrived' — does this mean 'she asked him at what time (**quando**) he had arrived' or 'she asked him after (**ubi** or **postquam**) he had arrived'?

80

After my girlfriend had gone away I was unhappy.
postquam amica mea abiit, tristis eram.

3. Latin uses the *pluperfect* after **ubi, ut, simul atque (simul ac)** and **quotiens** when the action of the verb has occurred repeatedly in the past, i.e. with the meaning 'whenever':

Whenever I saw my girlfriend I was happy.
ubi amicam meam uideram, felix eram.

When the repeated action refers to the present or the future, Latin is likely to use **quotiens** followed by the appropriate tense of the indicative.

I shall be very happy every time that you come to Rome.
ualde gaudebo quotiens Romam adueneris.

4. The words **postquam** and **posteaquam** are frequently split in two, the first part coming in the main clause and the **quam** coming at the beginning of the time clause:

I left the city after my friend had arrived.
post ex urbe exii quam amicus meus aduenit.

---

before	ante(a)quam, priusquam
until	dum, quoad, donec
while	dum, quoad

(a) Time clauses introduced by 'after' express a fact, but those introduced by 'before' may express *either* a fact *or* a possible event that may happen and can be avoided. If the time clause contains such an idea of *purpose*, its verb goes into the subjunctive, following sequence of tenses.

I left the forum before my friend arrived.
e foro exii antequam amicus meus aduenit.

I left the forum before my friend could arrive. (i.e. to avoid meeting him.)
e foro exii antequam amicus meus adueniret.

In the last sentence the word 'could' does not really mean 'was able to'. Latin simply uses the subjunctive of the verb meaning 'arrive': 'before my friend *might* arrive'.

Like **postquam**, **ante(a)quam** and **priusquam** are often split in two.

Similarly, time clauses introduce by 'until' may also express either a fact or a possible event, and they follow the same rule:

I called him Castor <u>until I found out</u> his name was Pollux.
eum Castorem appellabam <u>donec</u> nomen eius Pollucem esse <u>cognoui</u>.

The girl cried <u>until</u> her parents <u>bought</u> her a new dress.
    (i.e. so that they would do so)
puella flebat <u>donec</u> parentes ei uestem nouam <u>emerent</u>.

(b) In English the word 'while' can either mean 'during the time that ...' or, far less commonly, 'exactly as long as ...'. In Latin the construction for the former meaning is **dum** with the *present indicative*, even within an indirect statement:

While <u>she was crying</u> I left the house.
dum ea <u>lacrimat</u>, domum reliqui.

When **dum** means 'exactly as long as ...' the verb goes into the *natural tense of the indicative*, which will regularly be the same tense as the main verb:

All the time that the poet <u>was reciting</u>, I was listening carefully.
dum poeta <u>recitabat</u>, attente audiebam.

(c) As well as meaning 'while' and 'until', **dum** (along with **dum modo**) can also mean 'as long as, provided that', and in this meaning it is followed by a *subjunctive* verb:

Provided <u>you do</u> this, you will be safe.
dum hoc <u>agas</u>, tutus eris.

---

cum ('when, since, while; whenever')

When the verb in a **cum** clause is in a primary tense, the verb is in the indicative. (Watch out for the concealed future, described above.) When it is in a historic tense, it is in the subjunctive: this will be either an imperfect or a pluperfect subjunctive, never a perfect one:

> *When you come to Rome, I shall show you the Colosseum.*
> **cum Romam adueneris, Colosseum tibi monstrabo.**

> *When my son (had) arrived, we climbed the Capitol.*
> **cum filius meus aduenisset, Capitolium ascendimus.**

> *When (or while) I was riding with my friends, I told them the story.*
> **cum equitarem cum amicis, fabulam eis narraui.**

However, if there is a temporal adverb such as **tum**, **tunc** ('then'), **nunc**, **iam** ('now') or some other temporal expression, e.g. involving such words as **tempus** ('time') or **dies** ('day') in the main clause, a historic tense of the indicative may be used in the **cum** clause. (The clause will be purely a matter of time, without any other implications.)

> *Remember that time when Curio was lying in bed grieving.*
> **recordare tempus illud cum Curio maerens in lecto iacebat.**

notanda

1. Inverted **cum**:

Clauses with **cum** typically contain background information. If this information is in the main clause and the **cum** clause contains the principal action of the sentence, the indicative is used after **cum**, and the **cum** clause comes second:

> *The sun was rising when I left the town.*
> **sol oriebatur cum ex oppido exii.**

This is often used for unexpected events:

> *Hannibal was already at the walls when the Romans suddenly broke out.*
> **Hannibal iam subibat muros cum repente eruperunt Romani.**

2. **cum** + 'perfective' indicative = 'whenever, as often as'

> *whenever I shall cry*   (future time → future perfect indicative)
> **cum lacrimauero**

> *whenever I cry*   (present time → perfect indicative)
> **cum lacrimaui**

whenever I cried   (past time → pluperfect indicative)
cum lacrimaueram

3. **cum** meaning 'although' is always followed by the subjunctive.

Although Caelius <u>could have beaten</u> me, he let me win.
Caelius, cum me superare <u>posset,</u> tamen me uincere siuit.

It is sensible to put **tamen** at the head of the main clause to bring out the fact that the meaning of **cum** is 'although'.

Note that 'while' in English can be used to mean 'although', e.g. 'while you say that, I still say this'. It is important to distinguish this from the temporal use of 'while'.

✐ Exercises

A

1 When my friend had sailed to Greece, I was very sad.
2 While he was sailing to Greece, he was very sick.
3 When you arrive in Rome, do not forget to visit me.
4 Since he saw the doctor, he walks much better.
5 I rejoiced when [*i.e.* as soon as] I reached the finishing line.
6 After you reach Athens, visit the Acropolis.
7 When I am reading your poems, I remember you.
8 Bring her to me as soon as you see her.
9 Ever since I saw her, I have loved her.
10 He left the room after I had finished my recitation. [*Split* **postquam.**]

B

1 I left the house before my wife could abuse me.
2 While [*i.e.* all the time that] she was crying, I was laughing.
3 While I was doing the shopping, I bought some tasty fish.
4 Don't go away until you have spoken to me!
5 I left the theatre before the play ended.
6 I was a respectable girl until I met you.

7 Do not leave the city before you have visited me!
8 I waited in the forum until my girlfriend arrived.
9 Whenever the student laughed, the teacher got very annoyed.
10 The moon was shining when the wolf howled.

C

1 When you work hard, I am delighted.
2 When he had set out from Athens, he walked many miles before finding his friends.
3 When you do this, I shall congratulate you.
4 He was mugged when he was walking to Capua.
5 I was going out of the door when my friend arrived.
6 Whenever you cry, I comfort you.
7 The sailors sang while the ship sank.
8 He left Rome at the very time that I arrived and returned as soon as I left.
9 Kill Caesar before he becomes a king!
10 Whenever you see Cornelia, be nice to her, so long as she is nice to you.

 Further practice

V

Summer was approaching when the enemy invaded the country of the king, because they wanted to obtain great booty. But after they had come[1] to the city, they were ashamed. They asked why they had broken faith with a king (who had) once (been) well loved by them. However, since they had taken up arms and were already there, they decided to stay. While the enemy thought about these things, the king came out of the city before they could attack it, drew up a line of battle and drove them away. After he had taken their general, he said, 'I am delighted to have conquered but it pleases me to spare you.' The general said that he was overcome by his great spirit and wept.

1. use impersonal passive

Purpose clauses

Purpose clauses in English tend to be introduced by 'to', 'in order to', 'so as to', e.g.

> *to visit*
> *I went up to London*   *in order to visit the queen.*
> *so as to visit*

In Latin they are most commonly introduced by **ut** ('in order that') and, in the negative, **ne** ('in order that ... not'). The present or imperfect subjunctive is used, depending on sequence of tenses (pp. 45–6).

Thus in Latin the above sentence would be:

Londonium adii <u>ut reginam uiderem</u>.

Note also:

> *She is leaving London <u>so as not to see</u> the queen.*
> **Londinio abit <u>ne</u> reginam <u>uideat</u>.**

Because the negative is introduced by **ne**, the following have to be learnt:

ne quis, quis, quid	in order that nobody ..., in case anybody ..., etc.
ne ullus, ulla, ullum	so that no ... (*the meaning is stronger than that of* **ne quis**)
ne umquam, ne quando	so that ... never
ne usquam, necubi	so that ... nowhere

> *I burnt the book <u>so that no one</u> could read it.*
> **librum incendi <u>ne quis</u> eum legeret.**

neu or **neue** introduces a second purpose clause that is negative.

> *I am leaving the house so that my wife cannot see me <u>or</u> insult me.*
> **domum relinquo ne uxor me uideat <u>neu</u> uituperet.**

It would probably be a mistake to translate the word 'can' by **possum** in this sentence. The word is in effect part of the English subjunctive: 'so that my wife *may* not see ...'. When writing Latin purpose clauses, it is often a useful first step to convert the English into a form containing 'so that ...' (if it is not already in that form), because this will enable you to see in what person and number the subjunctive verb should be: while English uses the infinitive 'to X' forms for purpose clauses, Latin prose *never* uses the infinitive to express purpose.

Note the following 'signpost' words for purpose clauses:

idcirco, ideo	for this reason
eo	for this/that purpose
propterea	on this account
eo consilio	with this/that intention
ea causa, ea re	for this/that reason

I am going off to my villa <u>with the intention of</u> reading lots of books.
ad uillam meam <u>eo consilio</u> abeo <u>ut</u> multos libros legam.

If a purpose clause contains a comparative adjective or adverb, **quo** is used instead of **ut**:

They hurried <u>so that</u> they could get to the city <u>faster</u>.
festinauerunt <u>quo celerius</u> ad urbem aduenirent.

quo is an ablative expressing the measure of difference, here communicating the difference that their hurrying made to their purpose, i.e. 'by which amount'. The comparative word must always come immediately after **quo**.

Other ways of expressing purpose

Relative clauses

The relative with a verb in the subjunctive (p. 29) can be used to express purpose, especially after verbs of *giving*, *sending* and *choosing*. There will never be a negative in these purpose clauses.

My father sent me four books <u>to read</u>. (lit. *which I might read*)
pater quattuor libros mihi misit <u>quos legerem</u>.

The supine

The supine (with the ending -um) can be used to express purpose after verbs of motion and verbs which imply motion.

> *I went to the city <u>to greet</u> the general.*
> **ad urbem adii imperatorem <u>salutatum</u>.**

Note the common idiom **cubitum eo** 'I go to bed'. **cubitum** is the supine of **cubo** 'I lie down, lie asleep'.

The gerund and gerundive, and the future participle

For the use of the gerund and gerundive to express purpose, see p. 111. For the future participle expressing purpose, see p. 24.

✐ **Exercises**

A

1–3 I sent my son to Rome to see Caesar. [*three different ways*]
  4 Milo was going to Greece to see the Olympic games.
  5 The conspirators left the senate house in order not to hear Cicero's speech and distress themselves.
  6 We sent scouts in all directions so that Ariovistus could not hide anywhere.
  7 Atticus is sending the book with the intention of pleasing you.
  8 Run so that Atalanta cannot overtake you.
  9 Pliny looks after his slaves well so that they will look after him well.
 10 The cook worked hard so that we could all have a good meal.

B

1–3 I am sending friends to Athens to find my wife. [*three different ways*]
  4 The slave hid himself so that he couldn't be found anywhere.
  5 I am reading this book so that I can find out more about Latin.
  6 Please hurry up so that we can reach the sea faster.
  7 Paula praised Horace's poems in case he got upset.

8 He fled to Greece so that no enemy could disturb him.
9 My girlfriend is sending me a beautiful tunic to wear.
10 You must help your friend so that he doesn't get lost in the city and
      go into a brothel.

C

1 The slave ran out of the house so that he could talk to the messenger.
2 My girlfriend ran (away) fast so that my wife would not see her.
3 The cat went to London to visit the queen. [*Use supine.*]
4 Cato is going home with the intention of visiting his grandfather.
5 I am smiling at my husband in order to persuade him.
6 The dwarves climbed the trees to see the spectacle more easily.
7 Sulpicia is leaving Rome so as to avoid seeing her sisters.
8 Clodia left Rome so that she could swim in the sea.
9 I wrote it down so (that) I wouldn't have to remember.
10 Come to Rome to avoid working in the fields and meeting farmers.

Conditionals

Factual conditionals

Conditional sentences in English are ones that contain a clause beginning with 'if' or 'unless'. This clause usually comes before the main clause but can come after.

If you are sitting comfortably, then I will begin.
If the boat has arrived, there is fresh fish.

Unless you work hard, you will not succeed.

Conditional sentences, like these, may express *facts*. In Latin, factual conditionals have an 'if' clause that begins with either **si** ('if') or **nisi** ('if ... not, unless') and that has its verb in any appropriate tense of the indicative.

If the slave killed the citizen, he will be punished.
si seruus ciuem interfecit, punietur.

Note that Latin does not usually use **non** as the negative in a conditional clause, except to negate a single word; instead **nisi** is used.

If you don't love me, I am sad.
nisi me amas, tristis sum.

Like any main clause, the main clause of any conditional statement may be a question or command.

If it is water and not wine you seek, why are you in an inn?
si aquam non uinum quaeritis, quare in taberna estis?

Factual conditional statements about the future in Latin tend to reflect the fact that the condition must have been fulfilled before the consequence can follow.

If I win the lottery, I will give up work.

As a result, the 'if' clause often contains a verb in the *future perfect* tense when the verb in the main clause is in the *future* tense.

If you pay attention, you will be able to answer the question.
si attenderis, respondere poteris.

This also happens when the main clause verb is an imperative:

If you go out, buy me some flour.
si exieris, eme mihi aliquantum farinae.

Hypothetical conditionals

As well as conditional sentences that express facts, both English and Latin can express conditions which suppose something for the sake of argument.

If he had not arrived at that moment, the thief would have got away.
If it were not raining, we would be enjoying a picnic in the garden.
If I were to win the lottery, I would give up work.

The things supposed may be either ones which did not happen, are not happening now, or are portrayed as unlikely to happen in the future.

☑ These *hypothetical conditionals* can be recognised in English by the use of 'would' or 'could' in the main clause.

In Latin hypothetical conditionals, the verbs in both the 'if' clause and the main clause are in the *subjunctive*, and their tense (usually the same in both parts) depends on when the things supposed would have happened:

PAST   *pluperfect subjunctive*
    If you had kept quiet, you would have appeared clever.
    si tacuisses, sapiens uisus esses.

PRESENT   *imperfect subjunctive*
    If she were rich, she would not be lacking a husband.
    si diues esset, marito non careret.

FUTURE   *present subjunctive*
    If we were to do business, my wife would never speak to me again.
    If we did business,
    si negotium agamus, uxor mihi numquam iterum loquatur.

The easy way to identify whether a conditional is hypothetical and, if so, which of these three patterns to follow is simply to ask yourself whether the English could be followed by a phrase like 'but you didn't' (clearly past), 'but she isn't' (present), or 'but we won't' (future). You might find it helpful to think of the Latin subjunctive in this construction as being 'one tense back' from the meaning (e.g. present subjunctive for the future, imperfect for the present).

It is possible for the two halves of a hypothetical conditional sentence to be in different tenses, as appropriate to their meaning:

If Gaius had not revealed the plans, we would not now be in danger.
nisi Caius consilia patefecisset, nunc non periclitaremur.

In past hypothetical conditional statements, the verb in the main clause regularly appears in the (perfect or imperfect) indicative if it is a form of a verb expressing *obligation* or *possibility*, e.g. **debeo**, **possum**, **esse** with a gerund/gerundive or fut. pple, etc. The reason for this is that the verb of possibility is doing the work of the subjunctive by supplying the meaning 'could' or 'would'.

If we had not been so afraid, <u>we would never have been able</u> to do such things.
talia numquam facere <u>poteramus</u>, nisi ita timuissemus.

notanda

1. Remember that after **si** and **nisi** the words for 'any, some' are **quis, quid** ('someone, anyone') and **ullus, a, um** ('any'); note also **sicubi** ('if anywhere'), **si quando, si umquam** ('if ever, if at any time') etc. See p. 55.

2. In connected Latin, the usual way to say 'but if' is **quod si**; however, if there are two parallel and contrasting conditions in sentences next to each other, **sin** or **sin autem** is used to mean 'if on the other hand ...'.

If you are well, I am well; <u>but if</u> you are sick, I must come to you.
si uales, ualeo; <u>sin autem</u> aeger es, ad te uenire debeo.

3. English 'even if' is often rendered in Latin with a conditional clause introduced by **etiamsi**; see pp. 100–1. Likewise, English 'as if' may be translated with **uelut si**; see pp. 101–2. Both **etiamsi** and **uelut si** may introduce either factual or hypothetical conditionals according to their context and, of course, are followed by the appropriate construction.

4. Note that, in English, 'whether ... or ...' is sometimes used to introduce conditional clauses. In Latin, such double conditionals are expressed by **siue ... siue ...** or **seu ... seu ...**

Whether Clodia loves Catullus or hates him, she is my wife.
Clodia, <u>siue</u> Catullum amat <u>siue</u> odit, mea est uxor.

5. Be very careful never to confuse an indirect question with a conditional clause in English: both may be introduced by 'if' or 'whether'. Latin *never* uses a conditional clause to express an indirect question.

The girl will ask if the sailor is handsome. [indirect question]
rogabit puella num nauta pulcher sit.

If the sailor is handsome the girl will ask his name. [conditional]
si pulcher est nauta, puella nomen eius rogabit.

6. In fact, the only place in which Latin sometimes uses a **si** clause but English does not usually have a conditional construction is to express the meaning 'in the hope that …, in case …', for which Latin uses **si forte** and the present or imperfect subjunctive according to sequence (i.e. as if it were a true purpose clause).

We resisted their charms bravely <u>in the hope of</u> avoiding scandal.
blanditiis earum fortiter resistebamus <u>si forte</u> ignominiam uitaremus.

I made a careful search <u>in case</u> I should find another gold coin.
diligenter quaerebam <u>si forte</u> alium aureum inuenirem.

7. English 'if' often has the sense 'provided that': this should usually be translated with **dum (modo)** and a subjunctive verb (see p. 82).

✐ Exercises

A

1 If they are tired, show them to their bedrooms.
2 If Marcus did not kill the senator, why is he blushing?
3 If an audience likes a recitation, no one falls asleep.
4 If you kept your head, you were braver than most.
5 Do not read this book unless you like scary stories.
6 If rabbits are playing in the fields, foxes begin to feel hungry.
7 If young men take regular exercise, all the girls love them.

8 If I was angry, I treated you unjustly.

9 Unless we are honest, no one trusts us.

10 If Aulus was (ever) able to help a traveller, he would give him food and drink.

B

1 Unless the girls are behaving well, their parents will stop them going out.

2 If Nero had not killed his mother, everyone would have praised him.

3 If they are still asleep, wake them up.

4 How many plays would Terence have written, if he had survived?

5 If you walked as much as you talk, you'd be at the forum by now.

6 If the emperor does not pardon Mark, his wife will reveal her affair (with him).

7 The merchants would not sell lobsters, unless people wanted them (they were wanted).

8 Had we not arrived in the nick of time, the lion would have escaped.

9 If my daughter were to fall ill, I would call for a doctor straightaway.

10 Caecilius would be horrified, if he knew you were here.

C

1 If anyone wants me, I'll be in my room.

2 Whether Acilius is eloquent or the judges are easily deceived, the defendant will still be convicted.

3 After the earthquake we ran into the street in case the building were collapsing.

4 Even if Fortunata were really grieving, she would still have to be exiled.

5 But if she were to repent, it would be possible for her to be recalled.

6 If you find my brooch anywhere, bring it to me.

7 If on any occasion a messenger brought good news from Gaul, we rejoiced; but if he brought bad news, we asked if there was anything amusing from Africa.

8 Why would the boys be lying unless they did pour water on the old man?

9 If God did not exist, we would have to invent him.

10 If you trust the philosophers, they can help you; if you don't trust them, write a book about philosophy yourself.

Further practice

VI (continuing from p. 73)

Intending to punish Psyche, Cupid in fact falls in love with her and whisks her off to a private paradise where he visits her only in the darkness of night. Hence she doesn't know who he is. Her jealous sisters implant in her head the idea that he may be a serpent planning to devour her.

Extremely disturbed by the warnings of her sisters, Psyche began to wonder if he had married a serpent.[1] 'Unless my sisters are deceiving me,' she thought, 'I am in great danger.' If her husband had not returned that night, Psyche would still be happy. But, because she had been inflamed with anxious fear, she had hidden a razor with the purpose of killing him, and, when he was sleeping, she brought out the razor and a lamp which she had also hidden. She then saw that her husband was that most sweet god Cupid, and, thoroughly frightened, she decided to kill herself. This she would have done, had not the razor slipped from her hand. At length she began to love the husband whom she could now see. 'I would die if he left me,' she thought.

1. Latin prefers to launch the sentence with the subject, especially if it is a name. Compare English: 'When he had crossed the Rubicon, Caesar had cast the dice.' In English this could equally well be: 'When Caesar had crossed the Rubicon, he ...'. Latin prefers: 'Caesar, when he had crossed the Rubicon, had cast the dice.'

Result clauses

Result clauses are introduced in Latin by **ut** ('so that, so as to') or **ut non** ('so that not'). (A second result clause is introduced by **nec** or **neque** if it is negative.) The verb in the result clause is in the *subjunctive*. The subjunctive is in the tense dictated by the sense.

> *He is so sick that he is dying.*
> **adeo aegrotat ut moriatur.**

> *He was so sick that he was dying.*
> **adeo aegrotabat ut moreretur.**

Sense dictates the present subjunctive in the Latin result clause in the following sentence:

> *He was wounded so badly that he is dying.*
> **tam grauiter uulneratus est ut moriatur.**

To acknowledge the *completion* of the result, the *perfect* subjunctive is used. This is likely to be the case when the word 'actually' could be helpfully added to the English result clause.

> *He was wounded so badly that he (actually) died.*
> **tam grauiter uulneratus est ut mortuus sit.**

If a future meaning is needed, since Latin has no future subjunctive, you should use the future participle plus **sim** or **essem** depending on sequence:

> *She looks so beautiful in her new dress that all the boys will fall in love with her.*
> **tam pulchra in noua ueste uidetur ut omnes pueri eam amaturi sint.**

Note that in a result clause **se** and **suus** can only refer back to the subject of the result clause.

> *He praised Ovid so much that the poet (i.e. Ovid) showed him his new poems.*
> **Ouidium adeo laudauit ut poeta sua noua carmina ei ostenderit.**

Very frequently, indeed in all of the examples given above, result clauses are heralded by a 'signpost' word. Learn the following list:

talis, talis, tale	of such a kind, such
tantus, tanta, tantum	so great, so large
tot (*indeclinable*)	so many
totie(n)s	so often
tam	so (*with adj. and adv.*)
adeo	so much, to such an extent (*with verbs*)
tantopere	to such a great degree
ita, sic	so, in such a way

Note that the Latin for 'such a good man' is therefore *not* **talis bonus uir** but **tam bonus uir** ('so good a man').

A result clause can sometimes have a limiting force:

He is good in so far as he makes mistakes (only) from time to time.
ita bonus est ut interdum erret.

In line with the use of **ut non** as the negative of **ut** in result clauses, note:

ut nemo, nihil	that nobody, nothing
ut nullus	that no
ut numquam	that never
ut nusquam	that nowhere

notanda

1. For uses of the relative pronoun to express result, see p. 30.

2. Distinguish this use of English 'so (...) that' meaning 'with the result that' from when 'so that' means 'in order that' and introduces a purpose clause: 'I hid in such a way that I couldn't be found anywhere'.

3. Four useful expressions meaning 'it happens that' are followed by result clauses: **accidit ut**, **contingit ut**, **euenit ut**, **fit ut**. A result clause is also used with **efficio ut** 'I bring it about that'.

Exercises

A

1 I fancy Clodia so much that I am always writing poems about her.

2 Atalanta ran so fast that nobody could overtake her. [*Do you need to translate 'could' with* **possum** *here?*]
3 The boy behaved so well that he was never punished by the teachers.
4 The athlete exhausted himself so much yesterday that he is lying in bed today.
5 Mark was so bored by the lecture that he went to the pub.
6 The doctor looked after the athlete so well that he is exercising himself again today.
7 Cerberus barked so loudly that all the ghosts were afraid and did not stay near him.
8 You are working so well that I can only praise you.
9 Speak louder so that the deaf man can hear you.
10 The boy is so idle that he is not going to go to the lecture.

B

1 She is not the type to avoid danger.
2 There are some people who do not love the Latin language.
3 Hercules is too brave to avoid the lion.
4 The victor deserved to be crowned with a laurel garland.
5 Is Cicero the sort of person I can trust?
6 The muggers beat up the young man so seriously that he died.
7 It happens that I am present in Rome.
8 The old man doesn't deserve to be insulted in this way.
9 Catullus loves Clodia so much that he can never stop thinking about her.
10 Antony fled from the battle with the result that Octavius won.

C [a mixture of purpose clauses, result clauses and indirect commands]

1 I told him to listen to me and not to run away.
2 Acme lingered in the street so that Septimius could see her there.
3 Are you the sort of person who likes poetry?
4 I advise you to leave the city so that Marius doesn't discover you here.
5 Falco investigated the matter so well that the murderer was caught.
6 You deserve to be whipped.
7 I am writing my poems to become famous.
8 He is too bad a poet to become famous.
9 Can I persuade you to look at my paintings?
10 The children are learning Latin grammar to avoid being punished.

Because, although, as if

Because

The Latin words for 'because' are:

> quod
> quia
> quoniam

If a reason is given as the *actual* one, i.e. if the writer believes it to be true, the verb in the 'because' clauses is in the *indicative*. If the reason is an *alleged* one ('on the grounds that'), then the verb is in the *subjunctive*, and the word for 'because'/'on the grounds that' is **quod**.

> *Cicero executed the men <u>because they had conspired</u> against the state.*
> Cicero uiros interfecit <u>quod</u> contra rem publicam <u>coniurauerant</u>.

> *Cicero executed the men <u>on the grounds that they had conspired</u> against the state.*
> Cicero uiros interfecit <u>quod</u> contra rem publicam <u>coniurauissent</u>.

Rejected reasons are introduced by **non quod** or **non quo** and, as you would expect in a counterfactual statement, the verb goes into the subjunctive. If the actual reason is then given, the new clause is introduced by **sed quia** and the verb is in the indicative.

> *I went to the country <u>not because I was</u> tired <u>but because I wanted</u> to see you.*
> rus abii <u>non quod</u> fessus <u>essem</u> <u>sed quia</u> te uidere <u>uolui</u>.

Note the following 'signpost' words, all meaning 'for this reason':

> eo
> idcirco
> ideo
> propterea

> *I went to the country <u>(precisely) because</u> I wanted to see you.*
> rus <u>idcirco</u> abii <u>quod</u> te uidere uolui.

Note the following verbs of *emotion* which are frequently followed by **quod** ('because ..., that ...'):

aegre †fero	I am sorry
doleo [2]	I am sorry
†gaudeo	I am glad
laetor [1]	I am glad
miror [1]	I wonder

☑ *Other ways of expressing 'because'*

cum meaning 'since', 'because' is always followed by the subjunctive (see pp. 82–3).

quippe qui and **utpote qui** meaning 'inasmuch as', 'seeing that' are always followed by the subjunctive (see p. 29).

> *I always try to avoid that boy, <u>seeing that</u> I hate <u>him</u>.*
> **puerum illum <u>quippe quem</u> oderim semper uitare conor.**

Although

Causes beginning with 'although', 'though', 'even though', 'even if' which deal with *facts* have their verb in the *indicative*. If they deal with *possibilities*, the verb goes into the *subjunctive*.

> *<u>Although I lived</u> near the senate house, I still arrived late.*
> **<u>quamquam</u> prope curiam <u>habitaui</u>, sero tamen adueni.**

> *<u>However fast you walk</u>, you will still be late.*
> **<u>quamuis celeriter ambules</u>, tamen sero aduenies.**

> *<u>However wise you may be</u>, you are still not making progress.*
> **<u>quamuis sapiens sis</u>, tamen non bene proficis.**

Observe the difference in meaning between that of the last example and 'Although you are wise ...'.

Note that **tamen** can be used in the main clause to emphasise the meaning of 'although'. It often comes first in its clause, as in the last two examples above. It may instead come as second word, as in the first one, when it is likely to throw emphasis on the first word, here **sero** ('late').

Factual 'although' clauses are introduced by:

> **quamquam**
> **etsi**
> **tametsi**
> **etiam si, etiamsi**

'Although' clauses dealing with possibilities are introduced by:

> **quamuis**
> **etsi**
> **etiam si, etiamsi**

If a subjunctive is to be used after **etsi**, **etiam si** or **etiamsi**, its tense will be chosen by the rules that apply to hypothetical conditional clauses (see pp. 91–3). This is because they contain the word for 'if'.

quamuis meaning 'however' can also be used as an adverb with an adjective or adverb, even without a verb.

> *However wise (he is), he still makes mistakes.*
> **quamuis sapiens, tamen errat.**

☑ *Other ways of expressing 'although'*

cum meaning 'although' is always followed by the subjunctive (p. 84). **tamen** will usually be used as the first or second word of the main clause to elucidate this specific meaning of **cum**.

> *Although you speak well, I want another lawyer.*
> **cum bene loquaris, alium tamen suasorem uolo.**

As if, as

Comparisons in Latin are introduced by such expressions for 'as if', 'as though' as the following:

> **sicut**
> **quasi**
> **tamquam, tamquam si**
> **uelut, uelut si**
> **ut si**

> **perinde ac (si)**
> **haud aliter ac** ('not otherwise than')

If the comparison is false, i.e. to some imagined situation, then the subjunctive is used. If the comparison is true the indicative is used.

Take the English sentence, 'You look as if you have been dragged through a hedge backwards'. The comparison here is almost certainly false – you have *not* been dragged – and in Latin the verb 'you have been dragged' will be in the subjunctive. However, if you *have* been dragged through the hedge (which is a possible meaning), the verb will be in the indicative in Latin. In point of fact, comparisons are very likely to be to imagined situations.

> *Thespis was praised <u>as he deserved</u>.*
> **<u>ut meritus est</u>, Thespis laudatus est.**

> *Thespis was praised <u>as if he had deserved it</u>.*
> **Thespis laudatus est <u>tamquam id meruisset</u>.**

☑ In general, Latin prose resists the use of metaphors, unlike English prose. When it does use them, it tends to insert **uelut** or **quasi** meaning 'as it were', 'so to speak'. We sometimes refer to this as 'apologising for a metaphor' but it would probably be better to say that it is simply a way of acknowledging one.

> *Those cities were snatched (as it were) from the jaws of Hannibal.*
> **urbes illae uelut e faucibus Hannibalis ereptae sunt.**

✎ Exercises

A

1 I will come to your recital because I like your poems.
2 Although I hate you, I shall still come to your wedding.
3 The goddess is worshipped because she is great.
4 However brave (you are), you will still run away from Medusa.
5 Though the task is difficult, I shall nevertheless perform it.

6 Because Quintus loved the countryside, he went to his Tusculan villa.

7 Antonius hated Cicero because he had been abused by him.

8 I am sorry that you said that.

9 Although you are my friend, I am asking you to go away.

10 Because my friend is ill, I must visit him.

B

1 The Athenians killed Socrates on the grounds that he had corrupted the young men.

2 Even if you (may) dislike your teacher, give him an apple.

3 Regulus was cruelly punished as if he had done terrible (deeds).

4 Give him a lot of money seeing that he is so wise.

5 However annoying you may be, I shall always welcome you at my villa.

6 You dislike me, not because I am bad but because I am clever than you.

7 Even if you hurry to Rome, the emperor will die before you arrive.

8 You looked (appeared) as if you had seen a ghost.

9 'I try to avoid the common people,' said Coriolanus, 'in view of the fact that they smell.'

10 I love you because you are wonderful.

C

1 Since you are unwilling to go away, I shall leave the room.

2 Because Clodia lived by the river, she was glad that Catullus had bought a boat.

3 However hard you try, you will never succeed.

4 Seeing that you are trying hard, you will certainly succeed.

5 Cicero often praised himself on the grounds that he had saved the republic.

6 Although he was a good man, Cicero was still slaughtered.

7 Stentor was shouting as if I were deaf.

8 I shall go to Delphi because I want to consult Apollo.

9 Even if you were very wise, I would still not obey you.

10 I trust nobody, however friendly.

Reported speech

Reported speech (often known by its Latin name 'oratio obliqua') is very common in Latin. We have already met individually all the constructions used for reporting main clauses. However, there are different rules for reporting subordinate clauses (i.e. ones which could not stand on their own as sentences in their own right, e.g. those expressing cause, purpose, etc.), which we explain below.

In Latin it is possible to report many sentences in indirect speech without needing a verb of saying in each; there is usually just one at the outset. Regardless of the length of the speech, each individual clause is reported according the appropriate rule.

Remember that within indirect speech **se** and **suus** most normally refer to the person speaking, although they can be used to refer back to the subject of their own clause instead (in which case **ipse** ('self') is then sometimes used to refer back to the speaker by contrast). **eum** etc. never refers to the speaker (p. 50).

Main clauses

In indirect speech, the accusative and infinitive construction is used for reporting *statements* (pp. 58–61). Reported *questions* and *commands* follow the normal rules for indirect questions and commands (pp. 64–6 and 69–71 respectively). In long passages of indirect speech, where a verb of saying is not repeated in every sentence, the **ut** introducing an indirect command is usually omitted.

> *And he told them: 'I am angry. Go away! Why have you come?'*
> *And he warned them he was angry. They should leave. Why had they come?*
> **quos monebat se iratum esse. abirent. cur aduenissent?**

Subordinate clauses

In indirect speech, subordinate clauses (time, cause, purpose, result, relative etc.) with finite verbs do *not* become accusative and infinitive clauses. Instead they retain their form but their verbs become or remain subjunctive: the tense of the subjunctive is made to obey the rules of sequence according to the tense of the verb of speaking.

> *He says he loves her because she is beautiful.*
> **dicit se eam amare quod pulchra sit.**

> *They said they had eaten before they set out.*
> **dixerunt se cenauisse antequam profecti essent.**

For reference, these are the transformations:

ORIGINAL VERB TO BE REPORTED		PRESENT SEQUENCE	PAST SEQUENCE
indic: plpf, pf, impf, fut pf subj: pf, plpf		perfect subj	pluperfect subj
indic: pres subj: pres, impf		present subj	imperfect subj
indic: fut	*usually*	fut pple + **sim**	fut pple + **essem**
[*in time and 'if' clauses*		fut pple + **sim**	imperfect subj]

Note in particular the future perfect indicative which you may be surprised to find becomes perfect or pluperfect subjunctive.

> *'After they pick the apples, they will be tired.'*
> **'postquam mala carpserint, fessi erunt.'**

> *The manager said that after they had picked the apples, they would be tired.*
> **uilicus dixit eos fessos fore postquam mala carpsissent.**

There are only two exceptions to the rules in the table above. One concerns conditionals and is dealt with below. The other is that **dum** followed by the present indicative retains the present indicative in all circumstances, even in indirect speech.

notanda

1. Subordinate clauses of indirect statement remain unchanged when reported:

> *Clodia said her brother knew that she was unwell.*
> **Clodia dixit fratrem scire se aegram esse.**

2. If a subordinate clause is not in fact part of what was said but an authorial comment, its verb does not go into the subjunctive.

Mark was holding a book. 'Give me that book, Mark!'
Marcus librum tenebat. 'da mihi istum librum, Marce!'

Quintus asked Mark to give him the lamp, <u>which he was holding in his hand</u>.
Quintus Marcum rogauit ut sibi librum daret <u>quem in manu tenebat</u>.

Conditional statements in reported speech

Conditional sentences consist of two parts, a subordinate 'if' clause expressing the condition and a main clause expressing the consequence. In fact these two parts obey the general rules for subordinate and main clauses respectively.

When reported, therefore, the verb in an 'if' clause becomes or remains subjunctive: however, an existing imperfect or pluperfect subjunctive in a conditional never changes its tense even in present sequence.

The main clause of a conditional sentence has to become an accusative and infinitive as expected. In factual conditionals this follows the rules exactly as given for main clauses above.

'If you work hard, <u>you have</u> good luck.'
'si diligenter laboras, bona fortuna <u>tibi est</u>.'

<u>You know that</u> if you work hard, <u>you have</u> good luck.
<u>scis</u> si diligenter labores, bonam fortunam <u>tibi esse</u>.

More problematic is the fact that the main clauses of hypothetical conditionals are the only statements in Latin that can contain subjunctive verbs. Latin therefore needs a way to indicate that this is what is being reported. For future hypothetical main clauses, the present subjunctive is simply represented by the present infinitive. For present and past hypotheticals, the imperfect and pluperfect subjunctives both become a combination of future participle and **fuisse**:

'If you had worked hard, <u>we would have rejoiced</u>.'
'si diligenter laborauisses, <u>gauisi essemus</u>.'

> *They said that if you had worked hard, we would have rejoiced.*
> **dixerunt si diligenter laborauisses, nos gauisuros fuisse.**

Alternatively (and always for the passive or if there is no future participle), **futurum fuisse ut** is used followed by a subjunctive according to sequence.

> *They said that if you had worked hard, we would have rejoiced.*
> **dixerunt si diligenter laborauisses, futurum fuisse ut gauderemus.**

Exercises

A

1 Mark admitted he had been asleep when the teacher called his name.
2 When the teacher called his name again, Mark replied that he would try not to fall asleep a second time.
3 Even the first king did not know when the temple was built in the city.
4 Some people think Nero murdered his mother because he feared her.
5 No one told me you were in Syracuse to inspect the fleet.
6 Before they began to pray, the priests asked that we remain silent.
7 Several boys told me that they had read the books you had written.
8 The conspirators discovered that there was an entrance through which they could approach the emperor by surprise.
9 The architect says that the house will be finished in ten days, but I keep on telling him not to delay any longer.
10 The merchants knew that road to be dangerous and urged the pilgrims to avoid it.

B

1 The girls said they had come to the town to buy presents.
2 When Publius heard the bridge was finished, he decided to visit his mother, who was not well, more often.
3 Decimus hopes that Livia will marry him if he sends her frequent letters.
4 The young man told his girlfriend to arrive after his parents left, so that they would not know she had visited him.
5 We could see that the bull was running so fast that no one was going to catch it.

6 The farmer says that although he has many apple trees he doesn't like apples.
7 Surely you didn't promise that you would ride with him all the way to Vindolanda?
8 The citizens tell how every year there was a procession from the forum to the harbour.
9 I said no one would believe I baked that cake myself.
10 These boys think me a friendly girl, but they are mistaken if they think I like them.

C

1 The women said they had not bought anything because no one had given them any money.
2 Did you hear Stephanus is in Alexandria to be near his old mother?
3 They replied that after they watched the show, they returned to the house to rest.
4 The doctors say you are to stay in bed until you recover.
5 The guards explained that while everyone was asleep, several geese had been stolen but not the one that laid the golden eggs.
6 Our leader says that the enemy who have been threatening are no match for his best troops.
7 The emperor's freedman said that if Quintus couldn't stand the heat, he should get out of the kitchen.
8 The referee said that, when the trumpet sounded, every athlete should run as fast as possible towards the finishing line.
9 My painter knows that if he depicts his patron like a hero, he will be richly rewarded.
10 Gaius and Servius thought they would dig a ditch after they built the wall to prevent the river from flooding the new house.

Gerunds and gerundives

Gerunds

    I prefer <u>thinking</u> to <u>talking</u>.

The gerund is a verbal *noun*. In English it ends in *-ing*, e.g. 'doing', 'talking', 'thinking'. It is vital when one is looking at an English sentence to distinguish the gerund from the present participle, which also ends in *-ing* but is an *adjective*. Compare the gerunds in the example above with the participles in the following:

    The <u>thinking</u> man is wiser than the <u>talking</u> one.

If you are in any doubt, put the words 'the act (*or* action) of' in front of the word that ends in *-ing*. This will always make sense of a kind before a gerund but will be meaningless before a participle.

    Since it is an (active) *verbal* noun, the gerund of transitive verbs can take an object, e.g. 'reading <u>books</u>'.

    In Latin, the present infinitive supplies the nominative and accusative of the gerund, though the **-andum** (first conjugation)/**-endum** (other conjugations) form is used in the accusative after **ad**.

Nom. *<u>Walking</u> is easier than <u>running</u>. (<u>To walk</u> is easier than <u>to run</u>.)*
    <u>ambulare</u> facilius est quam <u>currere</u>.

Acc. *I like <u>walking</u> (<u>to walk</u>).*   *prepared <u>for fighting</u>*
    <u>ambulare</u> amo.   **paratus <u>ad pugnandum</u>**

Gen. *Cleopatra learnt the art <u>of ruling</u>.*
    Cleopatra artem <u>regendi</u> didicit.

Dat. *I have devoted myself <u>to teaching</u>.*
    <u>docendo</u> studui.

Abl. *<u>by reading</u> books*
    libros <u>legendo</u>

Gerundives

Gerundival attraction

The last Latin example above (**libros legendo**) is not, in fact, the best Latin. In English the gerund can take a straightforward object, but Latin prefers to *harmonise* the endings of the gerund and its object. This process is called *gerundival attraction*. It involves the use of the adjective of the gerund, the gerundive, which ends in **-andus** or **-endus** and declines like **bonus**.

This is how gerundival attraction works:

libros legendo   *by reading books*

The ablative obviously cannot be changed or a vital part of the meaning will be lost. Instead, the object of the gerund must be put into the case of the gerund, which in turn is made to agree with the noun:

libros legendo [→ *libris legendo*] → **libris legendis**

Likewise:

by loving the girl
puellam amando [→ *puella amando*] → **puella amanda**

Similarly **ars libros scribendi** ('the art of writing books') could become **ars librorum scribendorum**. In this last example, however, a further complication arises: some authors keep the gerund unattracted in the genitive plural of the first and second declension in order to avoid the unpleasing **-orum -orum** jingle.

Attraction should also be avoided (a) with neuter pronouns or adjectives in the genitive, dative or ablative, and (b) when the meaning of the verb is stressed.

The following nouns and adjectives are often followed by the genitive of the gerund or gerundive:

occasio, -onis *f*	opportunity
facultas, -tatis *f*	opportunity
signum, -i *n*	sign, signal
cupidus -a -um	eager
peritus -a -um	skilled

the signal <u>for going</u> to the ships
signum ad naues <u>eundi</u>

experienced <u>in riding</u>
peritus <u>equitandi</u>

The following verbs of giving and undertaking can be followed by gerunds or gerundives:

†**do**	I give
curo [1]	I see to
†**suscipio**	I undertake

I am seeing to <u>the education of my daughter</u>.
<u>filiam docendam</u> curo.

☑ Note these two common ways of expressive *purpose*:

- **ad** + the gerund or gerundive

    for the purpose of seeking peace
    ad pacem petendam

- The postpositions (prepositions placed after the nouns they govern) **causa** and **gratia** (both with the genitive) 'for the sake of' (see p. 38):

    for the sake of seeking peace, in order to seek peace
    pacis petendae causa

Gerundives expressing the idea that something should be done

The gerundive in Latin is in fact a *passive* verbal adjective. Combined with the verb 'to be', the gerundive expresses ideas of *obligation* ('ought', 'must', 'should', 'have to'). Look at the following English sentences:

Two things remain <u>to be said</u>.

This is certainly a movie <u>to be seen</u>.

The Latin gerundives **dicendus** and **uidendus** have the force of the underlined words. The meaning of the first sentence is that two more things *should* be said, and that of the second is that one certainly *ought* to see the film. In Latin a gerundive can be used with the verb **esse** to express obligation.

111

A. The gerundive of transitive verbs

I love the boy.
puerum amo.

The boy is loved.
puer amatur.

The boy is <u>to be loved</u>.
puer <u>amandus</u> est.

The agent goes into the *dative*:

The boy is to be loved <u>by me</u>.
puer <u>mihi</u> amandus est.

<u>You</u> must gather the flowers.
flores <u>tibi</u> colligendi sunt.

<u>He</u> must enter the town.
oppidum <u>ei</u> intrandum est.

Note that this pattern will only work with transitive verbs (verbs that take direct objects, see p. 74) since it involves making what was the object in English into the subject of the Latin verb.

☑ Deponent verbs form both gerunds and gerundives. Their gerundives are *passive* in meaning, like those of active verbs.

The deeds of Hercules are <u>to be imitated</u>.
Herculis acta <u>imitanda</u> sunt. (imitor [1] 'I imitate')

B. The gerundive of intransitive verbs (incl. verbs that take the dative)

With these verbs it is impossible to make the English object the subject of the Latin verb since (a) intransitive verbs cannot have an object and (b) verbs that have their object in the dative demand that it stay in the dative: it cannot be made the nominative subject of a gerundive construction.

The gerundive clause will therefore have to be expressed *impersonally* in Latin (compare the impersonal use of the passive, pp. 77–8). This means that you must rephrase the expression in English, starting with the word 'it' before you can translate it into Latin. The gerundive will agree with the impersonal subject: i.e. it will be neuter and end in **-um**.

We must go to Africa. (rephrased as *It is to be gone to Africa by us.*)
ad Africam nobis <u>eundum est</u>.

I must get up at sunrise. (rephrased as *It is to be got up by me at sunrise.*)
sole oriente mihi <u>surgendum est</u>.

Friends <u>must be obeyed</u>.
amicis <u>parendum est</u>.

As we have seen, the agent in this construction usually goes into the dative. If the last sentence had been 'you must obey your friends', and we were to translate it as **amicis tibi parendum est**, it would be unclear whether you should obey the friends or the friends should obey you. In such cases, **a** or **ab** with the ablative is used for the agent, i.e. **amicis a te parendum est**.

☑ **'without', 'instead of'**

A gerund or gerundive construction cannot be used to express 'without doing X'. Instead Latin can use an ablative absolute (pp. 21–3), a result clause (pp. 96–7), or, after a negative other than **non**, **quin** (pp. 119–20):

The people inside escaped the burning building <u>without anyone being hurt</u>.
qui intus erant <u>nullo laeso</u> ex aedificio ardenti effugerunt.

I regret having spoken <u>without thinking</u>.
me paenitet <u>ita</u> locutum esse <u>ut non considerarem</u>.

<u>No one</u> was permitted to visit the poet <u>without hearing his poetry</u>.
<u>nulli</u> licebat poetam uisitare <u>quin carmina eius audiret</u>.

Latin cannot use a gerund or gerundive construction for 'instead of doing X' either; a clause expressing 'although' is used instead (pp. 100–1):

<u>Instead of looking for</u> a horse, Tiro decided to walk home.
  (lit. *Although he could have looked for a horse ...*)
Tiro <u>cum</u> equum <u>quaerere potuisset</u> tamen domum ambulare constituit.

✐ Exercises

A [gerunds]

1 Orpheus loves singing.
2 Orpheus attracts the wild beasts by singing.
3 I went to Athens to hear Nero. [*Use gerund.*]
4 With great joy the troops heard the signal to advance.
5 Please see to the building of my villa.
6 Cicero took the opportunity to flee from his villa.
7 Eager to read books, he went quickly to his library.
8 He devoted himself to breeding chickens.
9 By reading philosophy, I become wiser every day.
10 I spend the time in sleeping and eating.

B [gerundives]

1 I must set out quickly and reach the city before sunset.
2 We must all forgive our enemies.
3 This girl should be avoided by all sensible boys.
4 We must leave Rome and make for Capua.
5 We must spend our time in drinking and making merry.
6 Soldiers should obey their generals and the generals ought to obey
   Caesar.
7 You should do some things and neglect others.
8 We must summon Cincinnatus in order to save Rome.
9 You must hurry to Rome and I must stay in Capua.
10 Clodia must find another man fast.

C [gerunds and gerundives]

1 One man restored the state for us by delaying.
2 'Tis you must go and I must bide.
3 You must persuade the Furies by singing.
4 Balbus saw to the building of the wall.
5 I am more fond of making love than of building walls.
6 Horatius must save Rome by defending the bridge.
7 I gave my girlfriend a book to read.
8 (Being) experienced in teaching, the master explained everything well.
9 Nausicaa gave Ulysses clothes to put on.
10 By studying hard, I make good progress.

Further practice

VII (continuing from p. 95)

Cupid and Psyche are separated but then reunited. Venus, however, is against the match and sets Psyche a series of ordeals. One of these is to separate out a huge pile of mixed up grains. A friendly ant volunteers her assistance.

Overcome by grief, Psyche despaired. 'What must I do,' she said, 'in order to carry out Venus' instructions? This task is so difficult that I cannot do it.' She was so upset that she fell to the ground weeping. But a friendly ant came to help her. 'Psyche,' she said, 'Venus has assigned you a great task but I shall help you. I shall see to the carrying out of her orders. I must help you and you must obey me.' Psyche was glad that the ant was so friendly.

VIII

The Carthaginians reach the top of the Alps

On the ninth day they reached[1] the mountain pass. When Hannibal had pitched camp there, (a chance to) rest was given to the soldiers, (who were) tired (out) with labouring and fighting. 'You must regain your strength,' said Hannibal to his men. But then a fall of snow increased their fear. Therefore, when Hannibal saw desperation on the faces of all (his men), he led them onto a ledge from which they were able to see the plains around the river Po.[2] And he said that they were climbing the walls not only of Italy but also of Rome, and if they kept their courage, they would soon have that city in their power.

(based on Livy 21.35.4–9)

1. 'it was come to'
2. 'around the river Po' = **Circumpadanus, a, um**

115

Verbs of fearing

Verbs of fearing can take a direct object:

Surely you aren't afraid of spiders?
num times araneas?

When English uses an infinitive after a verb of fearing, Latin uses one too:

I am afraid to fight with Milo.
timeo cum Milone certare.

When in English the word 'that' follows (or can be understood) after a verb of fearing, Latin uses **ne** plus the subjunctive. This apparently negative form is used because the person feeling the fear hopes that what he or she fears will *not* happen: cf. old-fashioned English 'lest'.

He is afraid (that) he may die.
timet ne moriatur.

Note that the English of this sentence could equally well have been 'He is afraid of dying.' If you recast the English ensuring that the word 'that' (**ne**) follows the verb of fearing, it should go easily into Latin.

The tense of the subjunctive follows sequence of tenses (see pp. 45–6). The present subjunctive can refer to the future in primary sequence and the imperfect subjunctive can refer to the future in historic sequence.

They are afraid that the enemy may conquer.
timent ne hostes superent.

I was afraid that you might lead my girlfriend astray.
timebam ne amicam meam corrumperes.

The Latin in the fear clauses could refer to the present as well as the future (e.g. 'that the enemy is conquering', 'that you are leading ...'). However, fears usually do refer to the future.

Fears for the past follow the same construction, using the perfect or pluperfect subjunctive according to sequence.

116

I was afraid that <u>you had led</u> my girlfriend astray.
timebam ne amicam meam <u>corrupisses</u>.

In the fear clause construction, the negative of **ne** is **ne … non** (or **ne numquam**, etc.) or it may be **ut**. The latter is *never* used when the main verb is negative.

I am afraid <u>that</u> you may <u>not</u> be working hard.
uereor <u>ut</u> diligenter labores.

In fear clauses **se** or **suus** refer back to the subject of the main verb (see p. 50).

<u>Caesar</u> was afraid that the people would not offer <u>him</u> the crown.
<u>Caesar</u> metuebat ut plebes coronam <u>sibi</u> offerret.

Fear clauses are introduced by such words as:

timeo [2]	I fear, I am afraid
†**metuo**	I fear, I am afraid
†**paueo**	I am frightened, terrified
uereor [2]	I fear, I am afraid
ueritus -a -um	fearing
timor, is *m*	fear
metus, us *m*	fear
periculum, i *n*	danger

Note therefore the following phrases which can introduce fear clauses:

There is a danger that …	**periculum est …**
There is a fear that …	**metus est …**

☑ English sometimes uses 'I am afraid that' as polite way to express regret. Latin can do this too:

I am afraid my father has already left.
timeo ne pater meus iam discesserit.

———

✎ Exercises

A

1 Catullus was afraid that Clodia would leave him.
2 Publius is afraid that Corinna may not come to his room at midday.
3 There was a danger that Boudicca might attack London.
4 Fearing that I might arrive too late, I hired a chariot to get to Rome.
5 Catullus was afraid to go to Asia.
6 Ulysses was terrified of Polyphemus' discovering him.
7 Cleopatra was not afraid to kill herself.
8 There is a fear that it may be unsafe to visit Egypt.
9 I am afraid that you have not come to praise me but to bury me.
10 The emperor is terrified that his wife will find out what he is doing.

B [fear clauses and other uses of **ut**]

1 I ordered my slave to find me a lion.
2 He went to Africa in order to do this.
3 When he reached Africa, he was afraid that he might not escape alive.
4 But he was not so cowardly that he fled.
5 My slave did not fear the lions as (he feared) me.
6 As he said, I am a very cruel master.
7 As he could not find a lion himself, my slave asked an African to sell him one.
8 When the African agreed, he bought a cage to bring the lion home.
9 He found sailors so brave that they were willing to carry the lion.
10 When my slave arrived with the lion, I was so happy that I freed him.

C [fear clauses and other uses of **ne**]

1 I fled to Gaul in order not to be conscripted.
2 Let's not worry about our Latin grammar!
3 I am afraid that my teacher may punish me.
4 There is a fear that Catullus may write nasty poems about Clodia.
5 Do not abuse your mother, my son!
6 Caesar told his troops not to be frightened.
7 I hid in the woods to avoid being hurt.
8 There's a danger that Caesar will not defeat Pompey.
9 The teacher encouraged Mark not to despair about his work.
10 Don't be afraid that I won't arrive in Italy.

quin and quominus

quin

quin is used after verbs of *doubting, denying, refusing, hindering* and *preventing* if they are *negatived*, i.e. used with a word meaning 'not', 'nothing' etc., or a 'virtual negative' e.g. **uix**, **aegre** ('scarcely'), or **num** introducing a question expecting the answer 'no'.

The verb in the **quin** clause will be in the subjunctive, its tense depending on sequence of tenses (pp. 45–6). Literally **quin** means 'by which not' but it often translates 'that' in English.

> *I do <u>not</u> doubt <u>that</u> you are intelligent.*
> **<u>non</u> dubito <u>quin</u> sapiens sis.**

> *She did <u>not</u> deny <u>that</u> she was visiting Catullus.*
> **<u>non</u> negauit <u>quin</u> Catullum uiseret.**

> *<u>Surely no one</u> doubts <u>that</u> you are a fool?*
> **<u>num quis</u> dubitat <u>quin</u> stultus sis?**

With verbs of hindering and preventing, the English is likely to continue 'from doing something', e.g.

> *I did not stop him visiting my sister.*

Putting this into Latin is problematic. To work in the old fashioned English 'but that' might be of some help: 'I did not stop him *but that* he visited my sister.'

> **eum non impediui quin sororem meam uiseret.**

You should master the following useful expressions:

- **haud (non) dubium est quin ...**   there is no doubt that ...

- **haud dubitari potest quin ...**   it cannot be doubted that ...[1]

---

[1] When **dubito** means 'I hesitate', it is followed by an infinitive.

119

- **haud multum** (*or* **minimum**) **afuit quin ...**
  almost, *lit.* it was not much (*or* very little) far from ...

  I was almost cut.
  haud multum afuit quin caederer.

  I was not much distant from being cut. (used personally)
  haud multum <u>afui</u> quin caederer.

- **non possum facere quin ...**
  I cannot help ...
- **non potest fieri quin ...**
  it is impossible that ... not

  That boring poet is bound to come.
  fieri non potest quin ille poeta molestus ueniat.

- **nemo est quin ...**
  there is nobody who ... not

  Everybody does this.
  nemo est quin hoc agat.

☑ After any clause containing a negative other than **non**, **quin** can be used to introduce a clause equivalent to English 'without ...'.

> *He <u>never</u> used to go to dinner <u>without</u> taking a present.*
> **<u>numquam</u> cenatum ibat <u>quin</u> donum afferret.**

---

quominus

quominus (literally, 'by which the less') is used after the same verbs and with the meaning much the same as **quin**, *whether the main verb is negatived or not*. It too is followed by the subjunctive, the tense of which depends on sequence of tenses (pp. 45–6).

> *I shall (not) stop you (from) seeing your mother.*
> **(non) te impediam quominus matrem tuam uideas.**

You should master the following common expressions:

- **per me stat quominus ...**
  it is due to me that ... not

  It is due to Brutus that Caesar did not become king.
  per Brutum stat quominus Caesar rex factus sit.

- **per me stat ut ...**   it is due to me that...

    It is due to Brutus that Caesar was killed.
    per Brutum stat ut Caesar interfectus sit.

☑ Note that **prohibeo** [2] ('I prevent') can be followed by the present infinitive.

    I stopped him <u>spitting</u>.
    eum <u>spuere</u> prohibui.

prohibeo can alternatively be followed by **ne**, **quominus** or (when it is negatived) **quin**, all with the subjunctive.

———————

✐ Exercises

A

1 It cannot be doubted that there were poets before Homer.
2 Jupiter will not stop me doing what I have decided to do.
3 I stopped Cicero from leaving Italy.
4 Cicero did not doubt that the legions were coming.
5 I did not deny that Cicero was a very great man.
6 Age did not stop the old man from loving young women.
7 Death does not deter (the) wise (man) from consulting the interests of the republic.
8 Antiochus did not refrain from writing a book against his teacher.
9 The winter storms will not prevent my coming to see you.
10 Don't try to stop me going to the theatre.

B

1 Surely no one can doubt that Virgil is an outstanding poet?
2 No one can deny that Virgil writes better poems than Horace.
3 It cannot be doubted that Homer is the prince of the poets.
4 I was almost suffocated by the heat at Baiae. [*Use* **quin**.]
5 It is due to his secretary that the letters of Cicero survive.
6 Everybody loves Antony. [*Use* **quin**.]
7 It is impossible that you are not studying my books.

8 It was down to me that he was working so hard.
9 I cannot help admiring Propertius' poems.
10 My teacher stopped me reading the poems of Horace.

C

1 Cicero couldn't help sending Atticus letters every day.
2 I must (*i.e.* I cannot but) cry out.
3 Fabius almost killed (*i.e.* came close to killing) Varus.
4 It is due to me that your son was not executed.
5 Don't stop me publishing poems about my girlfriend.
6 I do not deny that I have said bad things about you.
7 There is no one who doesn't like Latin.
8 My teacher is trying to stop me giving up Latin.
9 Nothing will stop me learning my grammar.
10 I do not doubt that Latin is a wonderful language.

Word order

Unlike English, Latin has a relatively free word order; that is to say, the order of words does not determine the grammatical role of those words in a sentence. However, this does not mean that Latin words can come in *any* order. There are many principles which guide and control the arrangement of words in phrases and sentences, and we look at some of these in this chapter.

First place topics and subjects

We are familiar with question words in English and in Latin coming first in their sentences. This is because they are, in loose terms, the *topic* or 'what the sentence is about', i.e. what the question is trying to find out.

> *Why did the chicken cross the road?*
> **cur pullus trans uiam ambulauit?**

We know that this is what the question is about because it determines what might be an appropriate answer ('to get to the other side').

In Latin, however, this principle applies not only to questions but to many other sentences too. The thing which comes first is normally what the sentence is about, whether it be subject, object, location, or even verbal action.

> *In the marketplace the citizens were listening to the many candidates.*
> **in foro multos candidatos audiebant ciues.**

This is a sentence about the marketplace: thus **in foro** comes first and is followed by what the sentence tells us about it.

Since in Latin subject personal pronouns are not needed for grammatical reasons, they are usually only put in for reasons of emphasis. By the same rule, typically they also need to come first in their clause.

> *It was you who told me the pretty girl is in love with me.*
> **tu mihi dixisti pulchram puellam me amare.**

Likewise, in a sentence containing a proper name of a person, particularly one who is the subject of the verb, this name is likely to be the topic:

> *But <u>Caligula</u>, not fearing the senators at all, always did whatever he wanted.*
> **<u>Caligula</u> autem senatores minime ueritus quodcumque uolebat semper faciebat.**

You can *sometimes* recognise topics by rewriting an English sentence to include phrases like 'it was X who ...' or 'Y was the one who ...' and seeing if the sentence still fits in the context. In these the topic is clearly separated from what the rest of the sentence says about it. If you come across an English sentence already in this form, it is usually possible to ignore the relative clause and simply use Latin word order to convey the meaning.

Adjectives and nouns

In Latin, adjectives can appear before or after the nouns they describe, even separated from them. The usual order is for adjectives (especially participles) to follow their nouns, but adjectives of size and quantity generally precede their nouns.

> *I put the <u>small</u> jewels into a <u>silver</u> box.*
> **in cistam <u>argenteam</u> posui <u>paruas</u> gemmas.**

A noun in the genitive accompanying another noun normally behaves like an adjective for the purposes of word order.

> *<u>Manilia's</u> father does not want her staying over with her friend.*
> **pater <u>Maniliae</u> non uult eam apud amicum nocte manere.**

Putting an adjective before its noun often emphasises it slightly or implies a contrast. In Classical prose the same also tends to be true for genitives.

> *A <u>general's</u> daughter cannot marry a slave.*
> **<u>ducis</u> filiae non licet seruo nubere.**

> *However, that girl doesn't know any <u>handsome</u> soldiers.*
> **tamen illa puella nullos <u>pulchros</u> milites nouit.**

Note that, in Latin, proper names can never be directly qualified by adjectives. Thus 'wicked Caesar' would be **Caesar homo nequissimus** and 'eloquent Cicero' would be **Cicero uir facundissimus**.

Prepositions

Latin prepositions almost always precede their noun phrases (pp. 33–8). However, it is not uncommon for a preposition directly to precede the noun it governs, separating it from a single preceding adjective.

> *The mother was sitting <u>in the middle of the hall</u>.*
> mater <u>medio in atrio</u> sedebat.

Verbs

Latin verbs tend to come at or towards the end of their clauses, particularly in subordinate clauses.

> *When I <u>lived</u> in Gaul, Livia <u>used</u> to visit me every time she <u>went</u> to Britain.*
> Liuia, cum in Gallia <u>habitarem</u>, totiens me uisitare <u>solebat</u> quotiens in Britanniam iter <u>faciebat</u>.

They may, however, come earlier, even first, if they are the topic of the sentence. This is common in direct commands, 'yes/no' questions, and other statements involving contrasts.

> <u>Have you had dinner</u> or not? — <u>Yes</u>, before I left home.
> <u>cenauisti</u>ne annon? — <u>cenaui</u> antequam domo discessi.

Notice how adverbs tend to appear next to the verbs they qualify. A good general rule in Latin is 'what goes together in meaning, belongs together in word order'. Departing from this rule (so-called *hyperbaton*) leads to a word order which lays emphasis on one word or another.

Second place unstressed words

In Latin, personal pronouns in cases other than the nominative are typically unstressed unless they are used emphatically and/or contrastively. Unstressed words should not appear first in a clause but instead usually appear as the second word in their clause.

> *You gave <u>me</u> the books.*
> libros <u>mihi</u> dedisti.

> *My sister helped <u>me</u>; she sent <u>him</u> away.*
> <u>me</u> adiuuit soror, <u>eum</u> dimisit.

The present indicative and infinitive of **sum, esse** behave similarly, except when they are stressed and/or do not have a complement, e.g. **cogito ergo <u>sum</u>** ('I think, therefore <u>I am</u>').

> *In Greece <u>there is</u> a city called Athens where the people once condemned a very wise philosopher.*
> **<u>est</u> in Graecia urbs, Athenae nomine, ubi populus olim philosophum ualde sapientem mortis damnauit.**

Some Latin 'words' can *only* appear in a second position, indeed attached to the word before them, rather like English 'n't', the unstressed form of 'not'. These are the question marker **-ne**, and the conjunctions **-que** ('and') and **-ue** ('or').

> *The boys <u>and</u> girls are at school.*
> **pueri puella<u>eque</u> in ludo sunt.**

Note also the phrase **ne ... quidem** ('not even') which appears to encircle what it emphasises:

> *I did a thing which I had<u>n't</u> done, <u>even as a young man</u>.*
> **feci id quod <u>ne adulescens quidem</u> feceram.** (Cicero)

> *<u>Not even the hungry</u> mice ate the old cheese.*
> **caseum ueterem <u>ne esurientes quidem</u> mures comederunt.**

Latin has a number of quasi-conjunctions which show the connections between separate sentences. Some usually come *as* first word in their sentence, others generally come immediately *after* the first word.

always 1st word	
nam	for (*introducing as a reason information not known before*)
usually 1st word	
itaque	and so (*in 2nd place only in writers after Livy*)
either 1st or 2nd	
tamen	however (*see also p. 100*)
igitur	therefore
ergo	therefore

always 2nd word

enim for (*introducing as a reason something known before, especially if common knowledge*)

autem, uero but (*a weak contrast with what precedes*)

'and'

Latin has many ways of saying 'and', with varying degrees of emphasis. The most common ways are to use **-que** (see above) or **et**. Note that **et** can mean 'also, too'.

Titus was walking in the garden <u>and</u> thinking about philosophy.
Titus in horto ambulabat <u>et</u> de philosophia secum cogitabat.

Latin also has the words **atque** and **ac**. These have exactly the same meaning, but **ac** is rarely used before a word beginning with a vowel or 'h'.

There will never be peace between men <u>and</u> gods.
numquam erit pax inter deos <u>atque</u> homines.

For 'both ... and', Latin uses either **et ... et ...** or **... -que ... -que** or **cum ... tum** (this is the conjunction **cum** *and not* the preposition which takes the ablative). 'Not only ... but also ...' is **non modo/solum ... sed etiam ...**

The slave girl was holding <u>both</u> a torch <u>and</u> a dagger.
<u>et</u> lucernam <u>et</u> pugionem tenebat ancilla.

<u>Not only</u> did she not trust the slaves <u>but also</u> a thief had previously attacked her.
<u>non modo</u> seruis non fidebat <u>sed etiam</u> fur eam prius aggressus erat.

For 'and ... not' etc., Latin *never* uses **et** followed by a negative immediately or later in the clause; instead **neque** or its shorter alternative **nec** is used.

My wife embraced me <u>and</u> did <u>not</u> hesitate to ask me where I had been.
uxor me amplexa est <u>nec</u> dubitauit me rogare ubi fuissem.

The boy fell from the horse <u>and no one</u> helped him.
puer de equo cecidit <u>nec quisquam</u> eum adiuuit.

When they heard this, they began to despair <u>and</u> they could <u>not</u> hide <u>anywhere</u>.
his auditis desperabant <u>nec usquam</u> se celare poterant.

After **nec/neque**, the 'any-' words are **quisquam, ullus**, etc. (p. 55).

'or'

Latin has many ways to say 'or'. **aut** or **aut ... aut ...** imply that the two options are exclusive and that they cannot both be right.

> *Either Cicero or Caesar can save the state.*
> **aut Caesar aut Cicero rem publicam seruare potest.**

Both **-ue** and **uel** imply that the two alternatives are interchangeable but say nothing about whether they may both be right, or at least imply that it does not matter.

> *My husband will be back from the country either today or tomorrow.*
> **uel hodie uel cras maritus rure reueniet.**

In questions, 'or' is **an** (p. 64); in alternative conditionals, it is **seu** or **siue** (see pp. 92–3).

> The Latin for 'neither ... nor ...' is **nec/neque ... nec/neque ...**

> *Neither in the forum nor on the river bank could the cook find fish.*
> **coquus neque in foro neque in ripa pisces inuenire poterat.**

> *I saw neither man nor woman in the city today.*
> **hodie nec uirum nec mulierem in urbe uidi.**

Indirect speech

Because the construction makes it clear that a sentence is reported speech (indirect statement, question, etc.), Latin has a tendency to slip into reported speech without needing a formal verb of saying to introduce every sentence. Even a mere implication of speech is enough. In reported speech, the subject of a statement in the accusative and infinitive must normally be expressed (p. 59): it typically comes earlier in the clause than the object, although this is not a hard and fast rule.

> *She asked if she wanted to go the games with her. Many gladiators were going to slaughter very fierce beasts.*
> **rogauit num secum ad spectaculum ire uellet. plurimos enim gladiatores bestias ferocissimas caesuros esse.**

☑ Note that **rogauit** here *precedes* the indirect speech rather than coming at the end of the sentence. This is normal for words introducing indirect speech.

128

Ablative absolute phrases

The noun and the participle in an ablative absolute phrase almost always encapsulate (i.e. surround) the phrase, any other words coming between them. The participle usually comes at the end of the phrase, though it may come first if the participle is the topic of the phrase.

> *After quickly writing a letter, I got up to look for some more wine. When I finally found the wine, I sat down again to read a book. Then, putting down the book, I fell asleep.*
> **litteris celeriter scriptis, surgebam ut plus uini quaererem. inuento tandem uino rursus consedi ut librum legerem. tum deposito libro obdormiui.**

The word order of most phrases involving participles follows the same pattern as that of ablative absolutes.

Asyndeton

Although Latin has many words for 'and', Latin authors sometimes chose to omit them for a more vivid effect. This is known as *asyndeton* (Greek 'unconnected').

> *The master caught the wicked slave, cursed him and beat him with sticks.*
> **dominus seruum nequam cepit, uituperauit, uirgis uerberauit.**

Latin writers found sequences of *three* parallel items like this (a so-called *tricolon*), with or without conjunctions, to be a particularly effective means of expression, especially if each one of the three parts is longer than the previous one (an *ascending tricolon*).

Chiasmus

Another elegant and effect trick of word order used by Latin authors (and occasionally English ones too) is the symmetrical pattern called *chiasmus* which involves reversing the expected order of words in the second of two phrases containing two ideas.

> *For three days the mother wept, her clothes torn, her hair dishevelled.*
> **tres dies mater ueste scissa passis crinibus flebat.**

129

The term chiasmus derives from the Greek letter *chi* (X) that may be formed by joining the 'parallel' parts of the phrase.

ueste		scissa
	X	
passis		crinibus

✐ **Exercises**

A

1 Watch the girl with the fair hair. She's the one I love.
2 Cunning Scipio easily overcame the Carthaginians.
3 Under the new bridge, several girls were swimming in the deep river.
4 Plautus' plays please me more than Terence's.
5 There were two lovers living in Verona who tragically died because their families were rivals.
6 Pliny was always worried about something; Trajan was often annoyed by Pliny.
7 The glass merchant carefully put down the phial.
8 In winter the dog would chase the cat; in summer it sleeps under the tree, (now that it is) leafy.
9 We were carrying water with us but we had to give it to the thirsty horses.
10 That tall building is the famous temple where wise priests and many faithful sailors pray daily to the powerful god Neptune.

B

1 Gaius says he obtained the food; (for) you were still sleeping.
2 The priest will pray to Minerva for you, if you bring a sacrificial animal to him.
3 Few people nowadays understand how the Greeks or Romans lived, and this is no surprise.
4 After all, if we admit Latin can be easily learnt, who will think us clever?

5 The sailor asked where I had come from: I could travel with him as far as Naples.

6 The Iceni pay their taxes. They expect that they will be treated fairly by you.

7 Wash not only my feet but also my hands and my face.

8 The steward was ordered to hire either dancing girls or dwarves; however, he hired both flute players and actors.

9 The master cursed his steward but praised the cook; for (he said) he had prepared an excellent dinner.

10 With great dignity the bereaved queen led me into the palace and told me of her sorrow. Not even the sweet words I spoke consoled her.

C

1 Surely the most powerful man in the world is not having an affair with his secretary? This shames the state: no man should behave with such dishonesty, dishonour and disrespect in his office.

2 I hear from my son that the countryside is very peaceful: apparently (*i.e.* he says that) birds fly over the trees, fish leap in the rivers, and lambs gambol without a care in the fields.

3 The prisoners were bound and judges summoned before we came in.

4 On the next day the young men and their girlfriends stayed at home, their parents being angry that they had been in the tavern.

5 We hold these truths to be self-evident, that all men are created equal, that they are endowed by their creator with certain inalienable rights, and that among these are life, liberty and the pursuit of happiness.

6 Do you remember Ennius? That poet knew how to tell a good story.

7 In no way do I defend the actions of my father, but his motives I cannot fault.

8 The banker said that I could only have a loan if I could prove I had enough money to repay him. Why then would I want the loan?

9 There was a dark cave near the shore of the lake across which we had sailed. We dragged the boat onto the shore and went inside in the hope of finding treasure.

10 There was a terrible drought and plague, and many were sick for a long time. No one knew who would reap the harvest even if the rain did eventually come.

Further practice

IX (continuing from p. 115)

Venus decided to prevent Cupid and the girl from meeting. She thought that in this way she could destroy their love. But Psyche was not the sort of person to despair easily. However, the commands of Venus were so terrible that she did not know what she was going to do; besides, nobody could deny that the goddess's power was very great. 'I hope,' she thought, 'that I shall find someone to help me.' And an ant and then an eagle came to her to give her help. She was worthy, as they thought, to marry Cupid, and Venus could not stop her from achieving this.

X

As she tries to execute one of Venus' commands, Psyche, through her own folly, ends up alone in the underworld in a deep faint. Persuaded by Cupid, Jupiter engineers a happy ending.

Cupid left his bedroom and flew to find the girl where she lay on the ground in a very deep sleep. When he saw her, he brought her safety.[1] Having awakened her with an arrow, he lifted her up and carried her to the palace of Jupiter, the father of the gods who considers the power of Cupid of very great importance, having suffered very many wounds from his bow himself. Venus was now persuaded by his sweet words to lay aside her anger and no longer to devise bad things against the girl. 'It is not (the part) of a true goddess to be angry with mortals,' he said. And so, when the gods had been called together, Psyche and Cupid were joined in matrimony and lived happily ever after.

1. use predicative dative (p. 5): 'was for a safety to her'

Latin prose style

In order to learn to write good Latin, it is vital first to read good Latin. We present here extracts from Latin prose authors to illustrate how they make use of the language to express themselves elegantly.

Cicero: Regulus

This fairly straightforward passage illustrates Cicero's characteristic stylistic order and elegance. After being captured by the Carthaginians, Regulus has been sent to Rome in the hope that he can arrange the ransoming of some of Rome's Carthaginian captives.

M. Atilius Regulus, cum consul iterum in Africa ex insidiis captus esset duce Xanthippo Lacedaemonio, imperatore autem patre Hannibalis Hamilcare, iuratus missus est ad senatum, ut, nisi redditi essent Poenis captiui nobiles quidam, rediret ipse Cathaginem. is cum Romam uenisset ..., in senatum uenit, mandata exposuit, sententiam 5
ne diceret recusauit: quam diu iure iurando hostium teneretur, non esse se senatorem. atque illud etiam ('o stultum hominem' dixerit quispiam 'et repugnantem utilitati suae') reddi captiuos negauit esse utile: illos enim adulescentes esse et bonos duces, se iam confectum senectute. cuius cum ualuisset auctoritas, captiui retenti sunt, ipse 10
Carthaginem rediit neque eum caritas patriae retinuit nec suorum. neque uero tum ignorabat se ad crudelem hostem et ad exquisita supplicia proficisci, sed ius iurandum conseruandum putabat. itaque tum, cum uigilando necabatur, erat in meliore causa quam si domi senex captiuus, periurus consularis remansisset. 15

Cicero, *De officiis* 3.99–100

M. Atilius Regulus (1)   Regulus is the topic of the episode: his name is placed at the head of the sentence (p. 124).

consul iterum (1)   'consul for the second time' (in 255 BC)

ex insidiis (1)   'as a result of an ambush'

duce ... Hamilcare (2–3)   Note the balancing ablative absolutes, with the participle 'being' having to be understood twice. The phrases are linked by **autem** in this accumulation of historical detail.

iuratus ... ut (3)   'on oath ... on condition that'

missus est ... redditi essent ... rediret (3–4)   Note the early positioning of the verbs. Ideas of motion are being stressed.

is (4)   The pronoun is used as a connection, as if it were a conjunction.

sententiam (5)   'his vote', emphatically placed outside the **ne** clause. **ne** is sometimes used as an alternative to **quominus**; **recuso** can also be followed by an infinitive.

quam diu ... senatorem (6–7)   Indirect statement with no introductory verb of saying (p. 128): one is implied by the context, however.

atque illud etiam (7)   'and what is more': **illud** looks forward to the main body of the sentence.

o stultum hominem (7)   accusative of exclamation (p. 2)

dixerit (7)   perfect subjunctive for a polite assertion: 'someone may say'

repugnantem utilitati suae (8)   'fighting against his own interests'

utile (9)   'expedient'

se (9)   referring back to the speaker, Regulus (p. 50)

cuius (10)   connecting relative: from now on the connections between sentences are clearly marked: **neque, itaque**. There is a smooth flow to the conclusion of the story.

ipse (10)   emphatic, 'himself, in person'

exquisita (12)   'carefully devised'

cum necabatur (14)   **necabatur** is in the indicative and not the subjunctive because the idea is purely temporal, with **tum** in the main clause (p. 83).

uigilando (14) 'by being kept awake'

senex captiuus, periurus consularis (15)   chiasmus, emphasised by asyndeton (pp. 129–30): the ideas are strikingly balanced.

Cicero: A good man

In this noble passage, Cicero pays tribute to Servius Sulpicius who has died while serving on an embassy to Mark Antony. The constant balancing of words and ideas that characterise the Latin here are so pervasive that we have not thought it worthwhile to draw attention to more than a bare minimum of them. They repay serious study.

uellem di immortales fecissent, patres conscripti, ut uiuo potius Ser. Sulpicio gratias ageremus quam honores mortuo quaereremus. nec uero dubito quin, si ille uir legationem renuntiare potuisset, reditus eius et uobis gratus fuerit et rei publicae salutaris futurus, non quo L. Philippo et L. Pisoni aut studium aut cura defuerit in tanto officio 5 tantoque munere, sed, cum Ser. Suplicius aetate illis anteiret, sapientia omnibus, subito ereptus e causa totam legationem orbam at debilitatam reliquit. quod si cuiquam iustus honos habitus est in morte legato, in nullo iustior quam in Ser. Sulpicio reperietur. ceteri qui in legatione mortem obierunt ad incertum uitae periculum sine ullo 10 mortis metu profecti sunt: Ser. Sulpicius cum aliqua perueniendi ad M. Antonium spe profectus est, nulla reuertendi. qui cum ita affectus esset ut, si ad grauem ualetudinem labor accessisset, sibi ipse diffideret, non recusauit quominus uel extremo spiritu, si quam opem rei publicae ferre posset, experiretur. itaque non illum uis hiemis, non 15 niues, non longitudo itineris, non asperitas uiarum, non morbus ingrauescens retardauit, cumque iam ad congressum colloquiumque eius peruenisset ad quem erat missus, in ipsa cura ac meditatione obeundi sui muneris excessit e uita.

Cicero, Philippic 9.1-2

uellem ... fecisset (1)   A potential subjunctive followed by a jussive subjunctive: 'I could wish that the immortal gods had granted...'.

ut uiuo ... quaereremus (1–2)   Study the balance of words and ideas in this clause. This will help you savour the many further instances of such balance which occur later.

renuntiare (3)   'report back on'

non quo (4)   a rejected reason (p. 99) with a subjunctive verb (5)

L. Philippo et L. Pisoni (4–5)   Philippus and Piso had been colleagues of Sulpicius on the embassy.

in tanto officio tantoque munere (5–6)   Balance lends emphasis. There is a difference in the ideas: **munus** tells us that the task was a burdensome one.

aetate … sapientia (6–7)   asyndeton

cuiquam … legato (8–9)   Translate together.

Sulpiciō reperiētur (9)   Roughly a third of the sentences in Cicero's speeches end in one of four rhythmic patterns. We call these 'clausulae'. The rhythm of the last six syllables of this sentence (–ᴗᴗᴗ/–ᵕ) was a notorious favourite of Cicero's.

The other famous clausulae are:

–ᴗ–/–ᵕ	e.g. **senātus populusque Rōmānus**
–ᵕ–/–ᴗᵕ	e.g. **uītae dēcēdere**
–ᵕ–/–ᴗ–ᵕ	e.g. **mentiō facta nōn est**

non … non … non … non … non (15–16)   The pile-up of obstacles is emphasised by this repetition at the start of the sense-units (*anaphora*) rammed home by asyndeton.

retardauit (17)   singular verb: each of the problems Sulpicius faced is taken individually with the verb.

meditatione obeundi sui muneris (18–19)   'preparation for performing his duty'

Caesar: The Nervii offer terms to the Romans

In Caesar's account of his campaigns in Gaul, he often has cause to report speeches made both by himself and other central figures in his narrative. Unlike English, where we would expect a direct speech report of the exact words used, Latin prefers indirect speech, and in this passage we see an extended example of a whole speech reported in this way.

At this point, Quintus Cicero, the orator's brother, is in command of a section of the Roman army, resting in its winter quarters (**hiberna**), that has come under siege from the Nervii, urged on by Ambiorix to take revenge and secure their freedom from the Romans. Cicero has already attempted in vain to get messengers through to Caesar seeking reinforcements, and the Nervii sense they have the upper hand.

tunc duces principesque Neruiorum, qui aliquem sermonis aditum causamque amicitiae cum Cicerone habebant, colloqui sese uelle dicunt. facta potestate eadem quae Ambiorix cum Titurio egerat commemorant: omnem esse in armis Galliam; Germanos Rhenum transisse; Caesaris reliquorumque hiberna oppugnari. addunt etiam de 5
Sabini morte; Ambiorigem ostentant fidei faciendae causa. errare eos dicunt, si quidquam ab his praesidi sperent, qui suis rebus diffidant; sese tamen hoc esse in Ciceronem populumque Romanum animo, ut nihil nisi hiberna recusent atque hanc inueterascere consuetudinem nolint: licere illis incolumibus per se ex hibernis discedere et 10
quascumque in partes uelint sine metu proficisci.

    Cicero ad haec unum modo respondit: non esse consuetudinem populi Romani accipere ab hoste armato condicionem; si ab armis discedere uelint, se adiutore utantur legatosque ad Caesarem mittant; sperare pro eius iustitia, quae petierint, impetraturos. 15

Caesar, De bello Gallico 5.41

colloqui sese uelle dicunt (2)   **dicunt** is a historic present: Caesar often uses this throughout the work, usually for a more vivid effect. Notice the word order: **colloqui** is what the Nervii want to do, and **sese** (acc. subject of **uelle**) is in second position after it.

Ambiorix cum Titurio (3)   In an earlier incident (5.36), Q. Titurius Sabinus had gone to Ambiorix to parley (his fellow *legatus* L. Cotta, who had been injured, refused to join him in this), accompanied by his tribunes and senior centurions. Ambiorix first ordered them to throw away their arms and then made a deliberately long speech — not quoted at that point by Caesar —, during which Titurius was surrounded and killed. Ambiorix used his success in the ensuing battle with the Romans to urge the Nervii to besiege Cicero's camp.

omnem esse in armis Galliam (4)   'It's all up in arms, Gaul': notice the balance and emphasis, with **esse** in second position.

Caesaris reliquorumque hiberna (5)   The new information here is about Caesar and the other troops; their camps are (falsely alleged to be) in trouble too, and hence they come first (Cicero and the reader already know that it is **hiberna** that are in trouble).

si quidquam ab his praesidi sperent, qui suis rebus diffidant (7)   These are factual conditional and relative clauses reported in indirect statement, with their verbs in the subjunctive as expected (pp. 104–6). After **si** we might expect **quid** rather than **quidquam** for 'anything' (p. 55); note the partitive genitive **praesidi**. Even in indirect speech **se** and **suus** can still refer to the subject of the verb in their own clause, as here (p. 50).

hoc ... animo (8)   ablative of description

in Ciceronem populumque Romanum (8)   **in** here means 'towards' and refers to Ambiorix' attitude, cf. the titles of legal speeches, e.g. **in Verrem** *Against Verres*.

ut nihil nisi hiberna recusent (8–9)   Result clauses retain their subjunctive verbs in indirect speech. Note the useful way of expressing 'only' as 'nothing except'.

licere illis incolumibus per se ex hibernis discedere (10)   Impersonal verbs like **licet** do not have a subject that can be expressed in indirect statement. **illi** here are the Romans, being offered a safe way out of their camp.

quascumque in partes uelint (11)   Relative pronouns and adverbs with **-cumque** on the end are indefinite ('-ever' in English). In direct statement they work just like normal relatives and usually take an indicative (p. 27). The subjunctive appears here not because of the idea of '-ever' but because the verb is in a subordinate clause in indirect speech.

non esse consuetudinem (12)   The emphatic denial **non** is put first.

si ... uelint, se adiutore utantur legatosque ... mittant (13–14)   The **si** clause is again that of a present factual conditional, and the subject is the Nervii (original words: 'if you are willing ...'). The main clauses have subjunctive verbs rather than infinitives because they are reported commands.

sperare pro eius iustitia, quae petierint, impetraturos (15)   Unexpectedly the subject of **sperare** is not expressed, but it is clearly Cicero (i.e. **se**); **spero** is generally followed by a future infinitive, here **impetraturos (esse)**, which also has no expressed subject but must refer to the Nervii. **quae petierint** is a relative clause in indirect speech and the antecedent **ea**

138

understood. The meaning of **pro** here is 'before' in the sense of 'in the light of', and **eius** refers to Caesar. Cicero thus throws the Nervii's offer to him back in their faces: if *they* surrender, Caesar may grant them their request.

Livy: The rape of Lucretia

Livy's extensive account of the history of the city of Rome from its foundation down to 9 BC demonstrates his mastery of elegant Latin style in writing history. The following extract from book I deals with a shocking incident from the end of the sixth century BC, one which also formed the basis for Shakespeare's *Rape of Lucrece*.

paucis interiectis diebus Sex. Tarquinius inscio Collatino cum comite uno Collatiam uenit. ubi exceptus benigne ab ignaris consilii cum post cenam in hospitale cubiculum deductus esset, amore ardens, post-quam satis tuta circa sopitique omnes uidebantur, stricto gladio ad dormientem Lucretiam uenit sinistraque manu mulieris pectore   5 oppresso 'tace, Lucretia!' inquit. 'Sex. Tarquinius sum; ferrum in manu est; moriere si emiseris uocem.' cum pauida ex somno mulier nullam opem prope mortem imminentem uideret, tum Tarquinius fateri amorem, orare, miscere precibus minas, uersare in omnes partes muliebrem animum. ubi obstinatam uidebat et ne mortis quidem metu   10 inclinari, addit ad metum dedecus: cum mortua iugulatum seruum nudum positurum ait, ut in sordido adulterio necata dicatur. quo terrore cum uicisset obstinatam pudicitiam uelut ui uictrix libido, pro-fectusque inde Tarquinius ferox expugnato decore muliebri esset, Lucretia maesta tanto malo nuntium Romam eundem ad patrem   15 Ardeamque ad uirum mittit, ut cum singulis fidelibus amicis ueniant; ita facto maturatoque opus esse; rem atrocem incidisse. Sp. Lucretius cum P. Valerio Volesi filio, Collatinus cum L. Iunio Bruto uenit, cum quo forte Romam rediens ab nuntio uxoris erat conuentus. Lucretiam sedentem maestam in cubiculo inueniunt. aduentu suorum lacrimae   20 obortae, quaerentique uiro 'satin salue?' 'minime' inquit; 'quid enim salui est mulieri amissa pudicitia? uestigia uiri alieni, Collatine, in lecto sunt tuo; ceterum corpus est tantum uiolatum, animus insons; mors testis erit. sed date dexteras fidemque haud inpune adultero fore. Sex. est Tarquinius, qui hostis pro hospite priore nocte ui armatus mihi sibi-   25 que, si uos uiri estis, pestiferum hinc abstulit gaudium.' dant ordine

omnes fidem; consolantur aegram animi auertendo noxam ab coacta
in autorem delicti: mentem peccare, non corpus, et unde consilium
afuerit, culpam abesse. 'uos' inquit 'uideritis, quid illi debeatur: ego me
etsi peccato absoluo, supplicio non libero; nec ulla deinde impudica 30
Lucretiae exemplo uiuet.' cultrum quem sub ueste abditum habebat,
eum in corde defigit prolapsaque in uulnus moribunda cecidit. conclamat uir paterque.

Livy, *Ab urbe condita* 1.58

paucis interiectis diebus (1)   We might expect Sex. Tarquinius to appear
first but this temporal ablative absolute marks the start of a new episode
about which we are going to hear.

inscio Collatino (1)   Putting the adjective first here lends it added force.

ubi ... inquit (2–6)   **ubi** here is a connecting relative (pp. 27–9), and it is
followed by several temporal clauses and phrases indicating the background leading up to the events, **exceptus ... consilii, cum ... esset, amore
ardens, postquam ... uidebantur, stricto gladio** etc. Notice how the length
of the sentence builds up tension and suspense with Lucretia unaware of
the events until the dramatic words **tace, Lucretia!** quoted in direct speech.

ad dormientem Lucretiam (4–5)   Participles are, of course, an exception
to the general rule that adjectives do not normally directly describe proper
nouns (p. 124). The present tense participle indicates that Lucretia was still
sleeping as this all happened.

moriere ... uocem (7)   Notice the emphatic placement of the verb at the
start of this future factual sentence.

tum ... fateri, orare, miscere ..., uersare ... animum (8–10)   In historical
prose, sequences of events, especially dramatic ones, can be narrated with a
sequence of 'historic' infinitives in place of verbs in past tenses or the
historic present. In reading it can be easy to mistake this for indirect
speech, but the subject here is nominative as it would have been with a perfect or present. The structure is not strictly a tricolon but notice the gradual
increase in length between the phrases **orare** and **uersare ... animum**.

necata dicatur (12)   In the passive, verbs of saying are generally used
personally with a nominative subject rather than impersonally with an
accusative and infinitive (p. 78).

uicisset obstinatam pudicitiam uelut ui uictrix libido (13) Latin authors often avoid using abstract nouns like **libido** as the subject of verbs denoting action because the personifying effect seems too vivid, but here the clause as a whole is a striking metaphor of conquest, appropriate to the narrative at this point. Still, Livy includes **uelut** with **uictrix** to soften part of the metaphor into a simile (p. 102).

cum singulis fidelibus amicis (16) As we can tell from the subsequent narrative, the use of the distributive **singuli** here indicates more than one individual in total (hence the plural) but only one each (p. 157).

cum ... conuentus (18–19) The relative **quo** forms part of the participle phrase (lit. 'while returning to Rome with whom ...', 'with whom he was returning to Rome when ...'). **conuenio** here is being treated as transitive.

quid enim salui (21–2) Note the partitive genitive use of the neuter adjective **saluum** with **quid** 'what of use/good'. **enim** here indicates that Lucretia expects them to agree with what amounts to a rhetorical question.

in lecto sunt tuo (22–3) Not obviously second in the sentence but, taking preposition plus noun as a single indivisible unit, a form of **esse** here is in the second position in a phrase. In fact, the vocative **Collatine** suggests that the sentence starts afresh before this phrase, the **uestigia uiri alieni** being the topic (NB also the shocking effect of the emphatic use of **uir**, when even **alienus** on its own would mean 'another man'): we might translate, 'The traces of another man, Collatinus, they are on your bed.'

ceterum corpus ... insons (23) The neuter singular of **ceteri** (otherwise used only in the plural) is used adverbially to mean 'but'; conjunctions usually do not count for calculating second position, so **est** here is in second position (see pp. 125–6; cf. **date** 24 in emphatic first position). Notice the parallelism and thus effect of contrast in **corpus ... uiolatum, animus insons**.

Sex. est Tarquinius ... (24–5) A clearer example of second position placement of unstressed forms of **esse** would be hard to find.

dant ... consolantur ... (26–7) Note the first position for these verbs because they are the topics of their clauses.

uos ... ego me etsi ... libero (29–30) Emphatic subject pronouns appear in first position, here put in because they contrast with each other (p. 123). **me**

is unstressed, appears in second position and can be understood with both
absoluo and **libero**.

eum (32)   This **eum** is grammatically unnecessary although not incorrect.
The effect here is to underline the topic status of the **cultrum**: 'the knife she
had hidden under her clothing, that is what she drives in her heart'.

conclamat uir paterque (32–3)   Agreement for phrases involving conjunctions like 'and' may be either with the whole (and be plural) or, far less
frequently, with the nearest subject, as here. The choice of the singular
underlines the fact that the two are portrayed as acting as one.

Tacitus: The death of Seneca

Tacitus wrote his histories in the late first century AD. This passage from
the *Annals* shows him at the peak of his powers. His style is compressed,
fitting much information into few words, and yet rarely obscure. In this
passage he describes the death of Seneca, who committed suicide in AD 65
at the command of Nero, his former pupil.

ille interritus poscit testamenti tabulas; ac denegante centurione
conuersus ad amicos, quando meritis eorum referre gratiam pro-
hiberetur, quod unum iam et tamen pulcherrimum habeat, imaginem
uitae suae relinquere testatur, cuius si memores essent, bonarum
artium famam fructum tam constantis amicitiae laturos. simul lacri-   5
mas eorum modo sermone, modo intentior in modum coercentis ad
firmitudinem reuocat, rogitans, ubi praecepta sapientiae, ubi tot per
annos meditata ratio aduersum imminentia. cui enim ignaram fuisse
saeuitiam Neronis? neque aliud superesse post matrem fratremque
interfectos, quam ut educatoris praeceptorisque necem adiceret.   10
   ubi haec atque talia uelut in commune disseruit, complectitur
uxorem, et paululum aduersus praesentem fortitudinem mollitus rogat
oratque, temperaret dolori neu aeternum susciperet, sed in contemplatione uitae per uirtutem actae desiderium mariti solaciis honestis
toleraret. illa contra sibi quoque destinatam mortem asseuerat   15
manumque percussoris exposcit. tum Seneca, gloriae eius non aduersus, simul amore, ne sibi unice dilectam ad iniurias relinqueret,
'uitae' inquit 'delenimenta monstraueram tibi, tu mortis decus mauis:
non inuidebo exemplo. sit huius tam fortis exitus constantia penes

142

utrosque par, claritudinis plus in tuo fine.' post quae eodem ictu 20
bracchia ferro exsoluunt. Seneca, quoniam senile corpus et parco uictu
tenuatum lenta effugia sanguini praebebat, crurum quoque et poplit-
um uenas abrumpit; saeuisque cruciatibus defessus, ne dolore suo
animum uxoris infringeret atque ipse uisendo eius tormenta ad im-
patientiam delaberetur, suadet in aliud cubiculum abscedere. et 25
nouissimo quoque momento suppeditante eloquentia aduocatis scriptoribus pleraque tradidit, quae in uulgus edita eius uerbis inuertere
supersedeo.

Tacitus, *Annals* 15.62–3

In a densely packed style like that of Tacitus very many things call out to
be commented on; we have made a selection of some of the most
interesting and limited ourselves to one or two examples of each. See if you
can spot further examples of these within this short extract.

ille interritus (1)   Here **ille** is used to mean 'the former' and refers (back) to
Seneca who was mentioned in the previous sentence; the alliteration here
(followed by **testamenti tabulas ... centurione conuersus**) emphasises the
contrast of his fearlessness with the fear of the man who had had to send in
a centurion to bring him the order to die.

poscit (1)   Throughout this passage Tacitus uses the historic present tense,
which gives the effect of vividly placing the reader there watching the
events unfold. A historic present may be followed by either present or
historic sequence.

denegante centurione (1)   Notice how throughout this typical passage
Tacitus uses subordinate clauses and phrases such as the ablative absolute
here and the following participle phrase **conuersus ad amicos** to convey
background information, using main clauses to focus on the key events.

simul ... rogitans ... imminentia (5–8)   This sentence is carefully balanced:
two phrases with **modo** ('at one time ... at another') are weighed against
two urgent indirect questions with **ubi** in which the absence of the expected
verbs **essent** and **esset** tallies with the question verb **rogitans** to portray
Seneca as not even finishing one question before starting the next.

cui ... Neronis? (8–9)   When a rhetorical question, i.e. one not expecting
an answer at all, is reported in indirect speech (which is here continuing
after **testatur**), it usually becomes an accusative and infinitive (rather than

143

an indirect question, p. 66). Notice the order **saeuitiam Neronis** with the genitive following the noun: **saeuitia** is opposed to other features of Nero that might have been observed, rather than Nero being opposed to other people who might have had **saeuitia**. Seneca's use of **enim** (p. 127) here also suggests he feels this was something well known to all. The use of **ignaram** here ('unknown' rather than 'unknowing') is unusual.

post matrem fratremque interfectos (9–10)   Where an adjective, such as a participle, describes two nouns of different genders, as **interfectos** here, it usually becomes masculine unless the two things are inanimate; sometimes, however, it agrees with the nearer of the two nouns. Notice how Latin uses adjectives where English would have 'of': 'after the deaths of his mother and brother' (p. 24).

educatoris praeceptorisque (10)   These nouns both refer to Seneca, described as Nero's tutor both academically and morally. Such a use of two terms for a single thing is called *hendiadys*.

in contemplatione uitae per uirtutem actae (13–14)   Note the objective use of the genitive (p. 8), and the encapsulated word order of the participle phrase (p. 129).

manumque percussoris exposcit (16)   A short main clause provides a arresting change and with it a dramatic sense of sudden progress in the narrative.

'uitae' inquit '... fine' (18–20)   The use of direct speech here adds a frisson of dramatic credibility to the depiction: if the reader were there, this is what would have been heard. Notice that **inquit** is second word in the speech.

uitae ... tu ... sit (18–19)   Typical examples of topic-first word order (pp. 123–4). Note especially the jussive subjunctive **sit** effectively expressing a command (p. 69).

fine (20)   Putting a word meaning 'end' at the end of the final set of reported actual words shows an elegant attention to detail.

Seneca, quoniam ... (21)   Since Seneca was not the subject of the previous verb, it is necessary to state the subject. Focusing on him by name here is appropriate to the narrative which is detailing his last actions, and since the narrative is about him, he is the topic appearing in first position.

ne ... atque ... (23–4)   We might expect **neu** instead of **atque** to add a second purpose clause here (as we had in 14 for the indirect commands **temperaret ... neu ... susciperet** where Seneca bids his wife to do neither of two separate things); the effect here is to imply 'so as not to do X and thereby accordingly not come to do Y either'.

uisendo eius tormenta (24)   Gerundival attraction is less common with neuter plural nouns in the genitive, dative or ablative (p. 110). Note that **eius** must refer to someone else's torments, i.e. his wife's.

suadet ... abscedere (25)   **suadeo** relatively rarely takes just an infinitive in classical prose ('he advises going into another bedroom'), usually preferring an indirect command (pp. 69–71) instead.

eloquentia aduocatis scriptoribus (26–7)   The ablative **eloquentia** expressing manner (pp. 9–10) functions like an adverb and thus comes next to the verbal form, which is put before the noun to emphasise it.

inuertere supersedeo (27–8)   Tacitus relatively rarely brings himself into the narrative by means of a first-person intrusion, but here this contrasts sharply with the use of **eius** (i.e. Seneca's) **uerbis**, which is set next to **inuertere supersedeo** and outside the phrase **in uulgus edita** where we might have expected to find it.

Longer passages

In this chapter we present passages that allow students to practise combining a range of constructions, together with some advice on writing connected Latin prose. We have tried to include in the Vocabulary the words which will enable students to handle these passages; however, since there is no 'right answer' in this kind of work, it would be sensible also to keep to hand a good dictionary which contains English into Latin.

Continuous classical Latin prose usually has a word at or near the start of each sentence connecting it to what came before. A list of such connecting words can be found on pp. 126–7. The connecting relative is frequently used, but be careful not to overdo this. Remember that relatives include such words as **qua** ('where') and **quo** ('to where'). Thus in XI below, 'while he was being carried there ...' can be translated **quo** ('to where') **dum ... portatur**.

If a logical connection cannot be found, a time word such as **tum** or **deinde** ('then') may be used. And do not forget about 'and'. It is often possible to put **autem** second word at the opening of a passage. While this word can mean 'but', it can also mean 'moreover' or 'now' (introducing a new idea) and so will fit most contexts.

However, Latin does not use 'and' to join clauses within sentences nearly as often as English does. It prefers instead to make use of subordinate clauses and participial phrases. Thus in XIV below, 'he called everybody together and announced ...' goes naturally into Latin as 'when he had called everybody together, he announced ...' or 'everybody having been called together, he announced ...'.

XI

When Cicero discovered that he had been proscribed by Marcus Antonius, he fled to his villa at Formiae near the sea.[1] He went to the harbour hoping to board a ship, but adverse winds stopped him from sailing. Now he was tired both of flight and of life and decided to return to his villa. 'I shall die,' he said, 'in the fatherland which I have often saved.' While he was being carried there in his litter, the assassins arrived. Although his slaves wanted to fight on his behalf, he told them not to do so. He ordered his litter to be put down and offered his neck to the assassins. They cut off his hands also because they had written against Antonius and sent them back to Rome with the head.

(based on Livy, fragment 50)

1. You have to write 'his villa at Formiae *which was* near the sea' in Latin. Otherwise the sentence will mean that his escape route was near the sea.

XII

Once a show of wild beasts was seen at Rome. All the animals were savage, but one lion was especially large. A slave of the consul was led into the arena to fight it. The whole crowd became silent because they wondered whether the slave would turn and run or fight with the lion. The lion, after approaching the man, suddenly stopped and then, embracing him, licked him with his tongue. All were so astonished at this that they shouted with joy.

XIII

Because I am an old man, I cannot walk easily. But once, when I was young, I was accustomed to wander in the mountains so that I could enjoy the pleasures of such a journey. I used to set out from home at dawn and at midday I often stood on the top of a mountain from where I could look at the pleasant countryside. If I had the strength, I would still do this. An old man, however, cannot do many things. He must sit in his garden reading a book and drinking wine, and he is lucky if his children come to see him. But, although this is true, I am a very happy man.

XIV

Once a king, who had three daughters, decided to divide his kingdom into three parts, and he called everybody together and announced that he would give the largest part to the daughter who seemed to love him the most. After he had spoken, the two elder girls said that they loved him more than life itself; but they were lying in order that they might get what they wanted. However, the youngest was not able to say what she felt because she did not wish to talk about her love of her father before so many people. The king was then so angry that he ordered her to go across the sea and gave his kingdom to the two other daughters. The youngest girl went away crying.

XV

Once upon a time, the god Dionysus, sad because Athens[1] had suffered so much, went to the Underworld in order to bring back from there a poet who might save the state. For the Greeks believed that poets gave the best advice. He had to go past many frightful monsters and he was certainly not the bravest of the gods. If a very faithful slave had not been with him, he would have fled to the earth. But at length he arrived at the house of Pluto, and when he had had a good meal, he asked him to show him the dead poets. Having delayed for a long time, he decided to bring back Aeschylus.

1. It is preferable to translate this as 'the Athenians': *people* suffered, not the abstract idea of a city.

If you have to put post-classical names into Latin, there are three ways of proceeding. First, if a Latin ending can be added to the name without making it sound too peculiar as Latin, add it. Thus Harold can become **Haroldus** and (in the following passage) Zadig can become **Zadigus**. Second, if you can think of a parallel situation in Roman life or history, you can transfer the whole prose to the ancient world. Thus the battle of Waterloo fought between Napoleon and Wellington could become the battle of Zama fought between Hannibal and Scipio. Third, if the reference is brief and unimportant in the context, you may simply substitute a suitable common noun, e.g. Oslo may become **urbs**, Chaucer just **poeta**.

XVI

Zadig is astonished at the reaction of Azora, his wife, to a scene of devotion.

Returning home angry one day, Azora said[1] to her husband, when he asked why she was angry, 'I was consoling a young widow who has been building a tomb for her husband near the stream at the edge of the meadow. She has sworn to stay by the tomb as long as water flowed in the stream nearby.' Zadig, her husband, expressed admiration at a woman who had truly been devoted to her husband. Azora, however, exclaimed, 'If only you knew what she was doing when I arrived: she was diverting the stream!'

(Voltaire, *Zadig or Destiny*, adapted)

1. Use indirect speech for the passage in inverted commas.

148

XVII

Candaules shocks Gyges, one of his guards, with an unusual request.

Candaules, who at that time was tyrant of Sardis, had in his bodyguard a guard named Gyges, son of Dascylus, whom he favoured greatly and with whom he used to discuss his most important business; and, being deeply in love with his wife and thinking her the most beautiful of all woman, he often boasted to Gyges of her beauty. One day, the king said to Gyges: 'I think you do not believe my words when I tell you how beautiful my wife is: well, since eyes provide better evidence than ears, you should see her naked.' Horrified, Gyges exclaimed 'Sire, what an improper thing it is that you propose! Am I to look on the queen without her clothes? Never, for, as they say, a woman without clothes is a woman without honour. Long ago, right and wrong were set apart, and it is only right for a man to look upon what is his own. Gyges said he had no doubt that the queen was the most beautiful of women but that Candaules should not ask him to behave so shamelessly.

(Herodotus, adapted)

XVIII

Zadig uses his trusted friend, Cador, to test his wife's devotion

A few days later Azora returned from the country and was told by weeping servants that her husband had suddenly died the previous night and they had buried him in the family tomb in the garden. She wept, tore her hair and swore to kill herself. That evening, Cador spoke to her and they mourned together. The next day, they dined together, mourned less and she began to admire him. During dinner, Cador complained of a pain in his spleen and said the only cure was to apply the nose of a man who had died on the previous day. Though Azora thought this strange, she believed her husband would still enter the next world even if his nose were to be shorter than in his first life. So she took a knife, dried her tears and made her way to Zadig in the tomb. Getting up, taking the knife and holding his nose, he said to her, 'Don't complain about the young widow so much! Your plan to cut off my nose is as bad as hers of diverting the stream.'

(Voltaire, *Zadig or Destiny*, adapted)

Latin often prefers to use concrete expressions where English uses abstract ones. Thus 'I replied to his question' may be best rendered in Latin as 'I replied to him asking', and 'I asked him the size of the army' may be rendered as 'I asked him how big the army was' (indirect question).

In the first sentence of XX below, 'refuse the king's demand' may be rendered as 'refuse the thing which (**id quod**) the king demanded'.

XIX

Candaules outlines his plan to enable Gyges to see his wife naked.

Although Gyges had tried earnestly to refuse the king's demand, because he was afraid of what dreadful thing might happen if he accepted it — the matter was bound to turn out ill in the end — Candaules, urging him not to become distressed, said there was nothing for him to fear either from him or his wife. 'I am not laying a trap for you,' he said. 'My wife will not harm you. Besides, I will see to it that she is completely unaware that you have seen her. You can hide behind the open door of our bedroom. My wife will follow me into the room, and she will place her clothes on the chair. You will easily be able to watch her from there before slipping away through the door as, with her back to you, she walks away from the chair towards the bed. Just take care that she does not catch sight of you!'

(Herodotus, adapted)

XX

Zadig, having now become a slave, aids Setoc, his master, to recover a bad debt

Setoc explained to Zadig that he had lent five hundred pieces of silver to a man before two witnesses and they were now dead, so the man refused to return the money. Asking about the circumstances of the loan, Zadig asked if he could plead the case before the judge. He told the judge that, although the witnesses were dead, he and the defendant could wait, and he would send for the large rock on which the money had been counted, because it would provide crucial evidence. When towards evening the rock had not yet arrived, the judge began to laugh. The debtor, also laughing, said the judge would have to wait until the next day at least; the rock was six miles away and would need fifteen men to move it. Zadig exclaimed: 'Behold the evidence of the rock! Since this man knows where it is, he proves it was on that rock that the money was counted.' And so the judge ordered that the debtor be tied to the rock without food or water until the debt was repaid, which it swiftly was.

(Voltaire, *Zadig or Destiny*, adapted)

English is fairly casual in its treatment of the order of events. Latin has a tendency to put them in the order in which they happened. Thus, in passage XXII below, the actual sequence of events is: Gyges cannot think of any way to avoid his master's bidding; he agrees to the plan; the time for sleep approaches; Candaules brings him to the room and hides him behind the door.

If you are worried in any way about the use of a Latin word which you find in an English–Latin vocabulary, look it up in the *Oxford Latin Dictionary*. In the passage below, it would be inappropriate to use **strido** or **strideo** to mean 'scream' since these are words largely restricted to Latin poetry and are hence unsuitable for prose. (If you see that Caesar, Cicero or Livy use a word, you need not hesitate to follow suit.) **allicio** is a good word for 'tempt', but for 'tempt to do something', you will discover from *OLD* that it needs to be used with **ad** or **in** + the gerund.

English idioms rarely translate directly into Latin. To render 'here and now' in XXII below as **hic et nunc** would create a very discordant effect. You can see if you can track down such expressions in *OLD* or in online resources containing whole texts such as Perseus (www.perseus.tufts.edu).

At this stage, you should probably be spending two to three hours on these passages, constantly checking the usage of words, phrases and clauses in dictionaries, and experimenting with word order. Your rough copy is likely to look a total mess!

XXI

Gyges spies on Candaules' wife and is faced with a terrible dilemma.

When bedtime approached, Candaules, since Gyges had agreed to the plan, finding himself unable to avoid doing his master's bidding, brought him to the room and hid him behind the door. Soon the queen arrived and began to undress, putting her clothes on the chair. When she turned and started towards the bed, Gyges slipped quietly from the room. She, however, at once realising what Candaules had done, did not scream or reveal her shame in any way, but instead silently resolved to take her revenge. At dawn she summoned Gyges, who often used to attend her and so came still unsuspecting that she knew what had happened in the bedchamber the previous night. 'Gyges,' she said, 'you have two choices open to you: either you kill my husband, seize his throne and take me as wife, or you die yourself here and now so that you are never again tempted out of obedience to the king to look at what is not yours to see.'

(Herodotus, adapted)

In England there is a long-standing tradition of Latin prose composition. In the past, great passages of contemporary oratory, such as Lincoln's Gettysburg address or Burke on the French revolution have been offered as a challenge to aspiring writers. The legacy of this tradition is a tendency to choose passages in now old-fashioned English. In these there is the added challenge of working out what the English means. For example, in the following passage of seventeenth-century English, 'undetermined' means that Crassus had not yet made up his mind; and today we would say that Ariamnes had received some kindnesses *from* Pompey rather than *of* him.

XXII

While Crassus was still undetermined, there came to the camp an Arab chief named Ariamnes, a wily fellow. Some of Pompey's old soldiers knew him, and remembered him to have received some kindnesses of Pompey, and to have been looked upon as a friend to the Romans; but he was now corrupted by the Parthian king's generals, and sent to Crassus to entice him from the river and hills into the wide plain, where he might be surrounded. For the Parthians did not want to fight with the Romans hand to hand. He therefore, coming to Crassus, admired the forces that Crassus had with him, but seemed to wonder why he delayed and did not use his feet rather than his arms[1] against men that had decided long ago to fly[2] to the Scythians or the Hyrcanians.

(Dryden, *Plutarch*, adapted)

1. *i.e.* 'weapons'   2. *i.e.* 'flee'

XXIII

Faced with no alternative, Gyges takes the throne.

So Gyges, presented with the choice of either himself killing the instigator of the plan or being killed himself for his shamelessness, for a little while was too astounded to speak. After begging the queen in vain not to force him to make such a choice, he chose to live and asked her how she wanted Candaules to die. 'Let us attack him,' she replied, 'as he sleeps, in the same room where he revealed me to you.' By nightfall all was ready, and the queen would not relent; handing him a dagger, she hid him behind the same door he had previously concealed himself behind. Then when Candaules was asleep, Gyges crept out and struck. In this way Gyges seized the throne and married the queen. However, the people took up arms, enraged at Candaules' murder; in the end the usurper's supporters agreed with them that if the oracle at Delphi declared him king, he should reign; otherwise he should give up the realm. The oracle was given in his favour, but, according to the Pythian, revenge for Candaules' death would come in the fifth generation (after Gyges). He later sent great gifts to Delphi, and he reigned for thirty-eight years, during which he did little else of note.

(Herodotus, adapted)

Since the following passage is highly rhetorical in the Cicero vein, you may like to see if you can include one or two of his clausulae (p. 136) in your Latin version.

XXIV

So judged those who were ignorant of the character and habits of the Spanish people. There is no country in Europe which it is so easy to over-run as Spain: there is no country which it is more difficult to conquer. Nothing can be more contemptible than the military resistance which Spain offers to an invader: nothing more to be feared than the energy which she puts forth when her regular military resistance has been beaten down. Her armies have long borne too much resemblance to mobs; but her mobs have had, in an unusual degree, the spirit of armies. The soldier, as compared with other soldiers, is deficient in military qualities; but the peasant has as much of these qualities as the soldier.

(Macaulay)

XXV

By my books some men have been inspired not only to read but also to write. Occasionally, however, I still fear that some good men despise the very[1] name of philosophy, and wonder that I give so much time and effort to it. For my part, when the republic was being governed by the men to whom it had entrusted itself, I devoted all my concern to it.[2] But when a single man came to rule everything, I found I had been excluded, and finally I lost my allies in preserving the republic, excellent men though they were. Then I did not give myself to the grief which would have over-whelmed me if I had not fought it, nor did I flee to pleasures unworthy of a free man.

(Cicero, adapted)

1. 'the name (of philosophy) itself'   2. *i.e.* 'I cared for it utterly'

XXVI

Gaius Pliny to his (friend) Caninius greeting.

I am one of those people who admires the ancient poets, although I do not – as some – despise the genius of those of our own day. For their tired and exhausted nature nowadays does not produce nothing worthy of praise. And indeed I have recently heard Vergilius Romanus reading for a few (friends) his comedy written in the style of old comedy, so well (written) in fact that it could some day serve as an example of them. I don't know whether you know the man, but you should. He is notable for the honesty of his behaviour, the elegance of his genius, the diversity of his works. He has composed verses with delicacy, flair and passion. He has written comedies in the style of Menander and others of his era. You may count these as being up among those of Plautus or Terence. Now for the first time, he has revealed himself in old comedy, but by no means as if he were a novice. That man lacked nothing in power, grandeur, delicacy, piquancy, sweetness, wit. He represents virtues in the fairest colours, and condemns vices; he makes appropriate use of made-up names and uses real ones when it seems apt. To sum up, I will grab his book off him and I shall send it to you to read and, what is more, to study. For I don't doubt that you won't be able to put it down once you have picked it up.

Farewell.

(Pliny, adapted)

Numbers and dates

Numbers

Cardinal numbers: 'How many?'

Cardinal numbers (**cardo** = 'hinge', the most essential part of a door) are the basic numbers used for counting: one, two, three etc. In Latin, cardinal numbers are adjectives; some of them decline to agree with their nouns:

- **unus**, **duo**, **tres** decline when alone and whenever they appear as part of a number ending in one, two or three:

  The boy was in love with two girls. He was afraid of the mother of one.
  duas puellas amabat puer. matrem unius timebat.

- the hundreds from **ducenti** to **nongenti**:

  The merchant imported eight hundred tables.
  mercator octingentas mensas importauit.

Latin numbers between 20 and 99 are formed *either* as in English (e.g. **octaginta septem** 'eighty-seven') *or* with the smaller number first, followed by **et** (e.g. **septem et octaginta** 'seven and eighty'): this second order is old-fashioned in English ('four and twenty blackbirds') but is perfectly normal in Latin.

The Latin for 1000, **mille**, is indeclinable:

Some say that there was an interval of 1461 (years).
sunt qui adseuerent mille quadringentos sexaginta unum interici.

(Tacitus)

However, for 2000, 3000, 4000 etc. Latin uses one of the following two constructions:

- the neuter plural noun **milia** ('thousands', which declines) is used with a cardinal number; the things being counted go into the genitive

  with three thousand books (lit. '*three thousands of books*')
  cum tribus milibus librorum

- indeclinable **mille** is used with an adverbial expression of how many times (see below)

with three thousand books
cum ter mille libris

📑 *notanda*

1. Numbers may be followed by a prepositional phrase instead of a partitive genitive (pp. 7, 33):

The officer set out with ten <u>of his centurions</u>.
legatus profectus est cum decem <u>ex centurionibus suis</u>.

2. **ad** is used with a number (usually without affecting the case of the noun) to express an approximation:

<u>*around*</u> *four thousand soldiers (were) killed*
occisis <u>ad</u> hominum milibus quattuor (Caesar)

Ordinal numbers

Ordinal numbers are adjectives used to express position in a list or order: first, second,[1] third, etc. In Latin these forms all decline.

The king executed his <u>second</u> and <u>fifth</u> wives. His <u>sixth</u> wife survived him.
rex de <u>altera</u> et <u>quinta</u> uxoribus supplicium sumpsit. <u>sexta</u> superfuit.

In ordinals over 10, all parts become ordinal (except **unus**) and decline:

in the <u>fourteenth</u> and <u>twenty-first</u> books of the Iliad
in <u>quarto decimo</u> et <u>uno et uicesimo</u> libris Iliadis

Other numbers

How many times?

Latin has number adverbs expressing how many times something happened; except for **semel** ('once'), **bis** ('twice'), **ter**, and **quater**, these

---

[1] The Latin for 'second' may be either **alter** or **secundus**. **alter** is used even in series that imply more than two members, and is regularly used as part of a compound (e.g. **alter et uicesimus** 'twenty-second'). **secundus** sometime has the force of 'second to something else', i.e. 'not-first' and by implication 'lesser, inferior'.

forms end in **-ie(n)s**, e.g. **uiciens** or **uicies** ('twenty times'). For numbers over 10, all parts become adverbs (including **unus > semel**). Being adverbs these words do not change their form to agree with anything.

How many each?

Distributive numbers express the meaning 'X number each':

> *The children received five denarii each.*
> **liberi quinos denarios acceperunt.**

They are always plural (even **singuli, ae, a** 'one each'):

> *The maids bought one lamp each.*
> **ancillae singulas lucernas emerunt.**

Latin has some nouns, like **castra** 'camp', which are plural in form: distributive numbers are used with these instead of cardinal numbers:

> *Caesar ordered two camps to be built near the river.*
> **Caesar bina castra prope flumen aedificari iussit.**

Fractions

Latin expresses fractions in a similar way to English, using cardinals and ordinals. A 'fifth' is **quinta pars**, and so 'four fifths' is **quattuor quintae** (**partes** being understood).

> *Africanus declares he has subjugated one third of the world.*
> **Africanus declarat tertiam partem orbis terrarum se subegisse.**

Latin also has some special words for fractions:

dimidia (pars) *f.*	half
semis, semissis *m.*	half
triens, ntis *m.*	one third
quadrans, ntis *m.*	one quarter
sextans, ntis *m.*	one sixth

Dates

In Latin the year is most often expressed by an ablative absolute phrase (pp. 21–3) made up of the names of the consuls for the year together with the word **consules**, e.g. **Sulla et Pompeio consulibus**.

The precise day is expressed in relation to the next of the three named days of each month, the Kalends (**Kalendae**, the 1st), the Nones (**Nonae**, usually the 5th), and the Ides (**Idus, -uum**, usually the 13th); these days are feminine and always plural in form. In four months the Nones and Ides were two days later:

In March, July, October, May,
Nones is the 7th, Ides the 15th day.

- If the date is one of these key days, the named day appears in the ablative (of time when, pp. 14–15) and the name of the month agrees with it

  on 15th March, on the Ides of March
  Idibus Martiis

- If the date is the day before one of these days, the word **pridie** is used with the named day in the accusative (with which the name of the month again agrees)

  on 14th March, on the day before the Ides of March
  pridie Idus Martias

- All other days are worked out from the next key day, counting backwards and including both the key day and the day being worked out: e.g. 17th January = 16 days before 1st *February*.
  The date is expressed with the formula **ante diem** with the ordinal of this number (agreeing with **diem**) followed by the key day in the accusative and *its* month name (again agreeing with it).

  on 17th January, on the 16th day before the Kalends of February
  ante diem sextum decimum Kalendas Februarias, a.d. XVI Kal. Feb.

☑ Dates were treated as fixed expressions that could be governed by prepositions, e.g. **usque ad a.d. VI Idus Martias** ('until 10th March').

✎ Exercises

A [Numbers]

1 The evil woman wanted one hundred and one dogs.
2 We saw thirty-three tombs built by the side of that road.
3 Near the first tomb fourteen prisoners had been crucified.
4 The king's daughter gave the dwarves three gold pieces each.
5 The priest walked around the altar ten times.
6 The teacher told the naughty pupil to write out the whole poem a
    hundred times.
7 Livy wrote one hundred and forty-two books about the Roman state.
8 Alcibiades received fifty talents each in taxes [*use gen.*] from the forts
    that Pharnabazus gave him.
9 About five hundred citizens were waiting outside the palace of the
    beautiful Egyptian queen.
10 On the eleventh day it rained for five hours.

B [Dates]

As you know, we left you on 2nd November, and we came to Leucas on
6th November, to Actium on the 7th. On 9th November we sailed from
there to Corcyra; we were at Corcyra until 16th November, held back by
the storms. On 27th November Cneius Plancus' slave at last brought (back)
to me a most welcome letter from you written on 13th November, which
greatly relieved me from my distress.

(Cicero, adapted)

The top Latin irregular verbs

In this list, forms beginning with hyphens are found in compounds (e.g. **-gredior** appears in **ingredior, progredior** etc.).

Present	Infinitive	Perfect	Supine	
addo	addere	addidi	additum	*add*
adipiscor	adipisci	adeptus sum		*obtain*
ago	agere	egi	actum	*do*
amplector	amplecti	amplexus sum		*embrace*
aperio	aperire	aperui	apertum	*open*
arcesso	arcessere	arcessiui	arcessitum	*send for*
audeo	audere	ausus sum		*dare*
bibo	bibere	bibi		*drink*
cado	cadere	cecidi	casum	*fall*
caedo	caedere	cecidi	caesum	*kill*
cano	canere	cecini	cantum	*sing*
capio	capere	cepi	captum	*take, seize*
carpo	carpere	carpsi	carptum	*pick, pluck*
cedo	cedere	cessi	cessum	*yield, give way*
cerno	cernere	creui	cretum	*perceive, discern*
-cipio	-cipere	-cepi	-ceptum	
claudo	claudere	clausi	clausum	*close, shut*
cognosco	cognoscere	cognoui	cognitum	*find out*
colo	colere	colui	cultum	*tend, worship*
consulo	consulere	consului	consultum	*consult*
credo	credere	credidi	creditum	*trust, believe*
cubo	cubare	cubui	cubitum	*lie down*
cupio	cupere	cupiui	cupitum	*desire*
curro	currere	cucurri, -curri	cursum	*run*
deleo	delere	deleui	deletum	*destroy*
dico	dicere	dixi	dictum	*say*
disco	discere	didici		*learn*
do	dare	dedi	datum	*give*
doceo	docere	docui	doctum	*teach*
duco	ducere	duxi	ductum	*lead*
edo	esse	edi	esum	*eat*
emo	emere	emi	emptum	*buy*
eo	ire	iui, -ii	itum	*go*
facio	facere	feci	factum	*do, make*
fallo	fallere	fefelli	falsum	*deceive*
faueo	fauere	faui	fautum	*favour*

160

fero	ferre	tuli	latum	*bear, carry*
-ficio	-ficere	-feci	-fectum	*do*
-fido	-fidere	-fisus sum		*trust*
fingo	fingere	finxi	fictum	*feign, pretend*
fio	fieri	factus sum		*become, be made*
fodio	fodere	fodi	fossum	*dig*
frango	frangere	fregi	fractum	*break*
fruor	frui	fructus sum		*enjoy, use*
fugio	fugere	fugi		*run away*
fundo	fundere	fudi	fusum	*pour*
fungor	fungi	functus sum		*perform, do*
gaudeo	gaudere	gauisus sum		*rejoice*
gemo	gemere	gemui	gemitum	*groan*
gero	gerere	gessi	gestum	*carry on*
-gredior	-gredi	-gressus sum		*go*
haereo	haerere	haesi		*stick*
haurio	haurire	hausi	haustum	*drain*
iacio	iacere	ieci	iactum	*throw*
ignosco	ignoscere	ignoui	ignotum	*forgive*
indulgeo	indulgere	indulsi	indultum	*be lenient to*
intellego	intellegere	intellexi	intellectum	*understand*
irascor	irasci	iratus sum		*grow angry*
iubeo	iubere	iussi	iussum	*command*
iungo	iungere	iunxi	iunctum	*join*
iuuo	iuuare	iuui	iutum	*help*
labor	labi	lapsus sum		*slip*
lego	legere	legi	lectum	*read*
loquor	loqui	locutus sum		*speak*
ludo	ludere	lusi	lusum	*play*
maneo	manere	mansi	mansum	*remain*
metuo	metuere	metui		*fear*
mitto	mittere	misi	missum	*send*
morior	mori	mortuus sum		*die*
moueo	mouere	moui	motum	*move*
nubo	nubere	nupsi	nuptum	*marry*
obliuiscor	obliuisci	oblitus sum		*forget*
orior	oriri	ortus sum		*arise*
parco	parcere	peperci	parsum	*spare*
pario	parere	peperi	partum	*give birth, bear*
patior	pati	passus sum		*suffer, endure*
paueo	pauere	paui		*be terrified*
pello	pellere	pepuli	pulsum	*drive*
peto	petere	petiui	petitum	*seek*
plaudo	plaudere	plausi	plausum	*applaud*
pono	ponere	posui	positum	*place, put*

161

premo	premere	pressi	pressum	*press*
proficiscor	proficisci	profectus sum		*set out*
quaero	quaerere	quaesiui	quaesitum	*seek*
queror	queri	questus sum		*complain*
rapio	rapere	rapui	raptum	*seize*
rego	regere	rexi	rectum	*rule*
relinquo	relinquere	reliqui	relictum	*leave*
rideo	ridere	risi	risum	*laugh*
rumpo	rumpere	rupi	ruptum	*break*
salio	salire	salui		*jump*
-scendo	-scendere	-scendi	-scensum	*climb*
scribo	scribere	scripsi	scriptum	*write*
seco	secare	secui	sectum	*cut*
sedeo	sedere	sedi	sessum	*sit*
sentio	sentire	sensi	sensum	*sense*
sepelio	sepelire	sepeliui, sepelii	sepultum	*bury*
sequor	sequi	secutus sum		*follow*
sino	sinere	siui, sii	situm	*allow*
sisto	sistere	steti, -stiti	statum	*stand, stop*
soleo	solere	solitus sum		*be used to*
soluo	soluere	solui	solutum	*loosen, release*
sperno	spernere	spreui	spretum	*despise*
-spicio	-spicere	-spexi	-spectum	*look, see*
statuo	statuere	statui	statutum	*set up*
-stituo	-stituere	-stitui	-stitutum	
sto	stare	steti	statum	*stand*
struo	struere	struxi	structum	*arrange*
suadeo	suadere	suasi	suasum	*persuade*
sum	esse	fui		*be*
sumo	sumere	sumpsi	sumptum	*take*
teneo	tenere	tenui	-tentum	*hold*
tollo	tollere	sustuli	sublatum	*lift, raise*
traho	trahere	traxi	tractum	*drag*
ueho	uehere	uexi	uectum	*carry*
uenio	uenire	ueni	uentum	*come*
uerto	uertere	uerti	uersum	*turn*
ueto	uetare	uetui	uetitum	*forbid*
uideo	uidere	uidi	uisum	*see*
uincio	uincire	uinxi	uinctum	*bind*
uinco	uincere	uici	uictum	*conquer*
uiuo	uiuere	uixi	uictum	*live*
ulciscor	ulcisci	ultus sum		*avenge*
uolo	uelle	uolui		*want*
uro	urere	ussi	ustum	*burn* (tr.)
utor	uti	usus sum		*use*

162

English–Latin vocabulary

This list is limited to the vocabulary needed to complete the exercises in this book. Nouns are given with their genitive and gender, adjectives with their (feminine and) neuter nominative singular. Verbs are given with their principal parts unless they are regular (in which case their conjugation is given in brackets) or they are (a compound of) a verb in the list on pp. 160–2 (in which case they are marked with a dagger †).

about   **de** + *abl*
abuse   **uitupero** [1]
accept   (agree to) †**con-sentio**
according to   **secundum** + *acc*
accustomed: be ~ to   †**soleo** + *infin*
achieve   †**ef-ficio**
across   **trans**; **per** + *acc*
action   **actum, i** *n*; actions **res gestae** *f pl*
actor   **histrio, onis** *m*
add   †**addo**; *see also* increase
address   †**ad-loquor**
adjacent to   **iuxta** + *acc*
administer   **administro** [1]
admire   **miror** [1]; **admiror** [1]
admit   **fateor, eri, fassus sum**; †**ad-mitto**
advance   †**pro-gredior**
adverse   **aduersus, a, um**
advice   **consilium, ii** *n*
advise   †**suadeo** + *dat of person, acc of plan*
affair   (matter) **res, rei** *f*, (liaison) **adulterium, ii** *n*; have an ~ with **adultero** [1] + *acc*
afraid   **territus, a, um**
afraid: be ~   *see* fear
after   **post** + *acc*; ~ all **nam**; **enim**
again   **iterum**; **rursus**; **rursum**
against   **contra** + *acc*; **in** + *acc*
age: old ~   **senectus, utis** *f*
ago   **abhinc**, *see p. 15*
agree   †**as-sentio**; †**con-sentio**; (make a bargain) **paciscor, i, pactus sum**
alert   (ready) **promptus, a, um**; (lively) **alacer, cris, cre**; (watchful) **uigil** (*gen* **ilis**)
alive   **uiuus, a, um**
all   **omnis, e**
ally   **socius, ii** *m*
alone   **solus, a, um**

already   **iam**
always   **semper**
also   **quoque; et**
altar   **ara, ae** *f*
amazed: be ~   **miror** [1]
ambassador   **legatus, i** *m*
ambush   **insidiae, arum** *f pl*
amphitheatre   **amphitheatrum, i** *n*
amphora   **amphora, ae** *f*
amusing   **iocosus, a, um**
ancient   **antiquus, a, um**
and   **et; ac; atque**; (in addition) **ad quod**; ~ ... not **nec; neque; neu(e)**
anger   **ira, ae** *f*
angry   **iratus, a, um**; be ~ with †**irascor**
animal   **animal, is** *n*
announce   **nuntio** [1]; (proclaim publicly) **pronuntio** [1]
annoy   **uexo** [1]
annoyed: become ~   †**irascor**
annoying   **molestus, a, um**
another   **alius, a, ud**
ant   **formica, ae** *f*
anxious   **anxius, a, um**
any, any...   *see p. 55*
apart: set ~   †**se-iungo**; †**dis-iungo**
appear   (seem) †**uideor**
applaud   †**plaudo**
apple   **malum, i** *n*
apply   **adhibeo** [2]
approach   **appropinquo** [1] + *dat*
aqueduct   **aquaeductus, us** *m*
arch   **arcus, i** *m*
architect   **architectus, i** *m*
archives   *see* files
arena   **arena, ae** *f*
arise   †**orior**

arms   (weapons) **arma, orum** *n pl*
army   **exercitus, us** *m*
around   **circum** + *acc*
arrange   †**con-stituo**
arrest   **comprehendo, ere, di, nsum**
arrive   †**ad-uenio**
arrow   **sagitta, ae** *f*
artist   **artifex, icis** *m*
as   (as if) *see pp. 101–2*; (while) *see pp. 81–2*; (since, because) *see pp. 99–100*; ~ soon ~ *see pp. 80–1*; the same ~ *see p. 54*; ~ well **et**; **quoque**; ~ often/many/much ~ *see p. 28*; ~ ... ~ possible **quam** + *sup*
ashamed: be ~ of   **pudet** + *acc of person feeling shame, gen of cause of shame*
ask   (question) **rogo** [1]; (~ to do) **rogo** [1]; ~ for **rogo** [1] **pro** + *abl*
asleep: be ~ **dormio** [4]; fall ~ **obdormio** [4]
assassin   **sicarius, ii** *m*
assign   **mando** [1]
astonish   †**obstupe-facio**
at   (of place) *see p. 16*; (of time) *see pp. 14–15*; (during) **inter** + *acc*; ~ last, ~ length **tandem**; ~ least **saltem**
athlete   **athleta, ae** *m*
attack *n*   **impetus, us** *m*
attack *vt*   **oppugno** [1]; †**ag-gredior**
attend   (accompany) **comitor** [1]
attract   **allicio, ere, lexi, lectum**
audience   **spectatores, um** *m pl*; **auditores, um** *m pl*
avenge   †**ulciscor**
avoid   **uito** [1]
awake: stay ~   **uigilo** [1]
awaken *vt*   **suscito** [1]
award   *see* decree
aware   **conscius, a, um** + *gen*
away: be ~   †**ab-sum**

baby   **infans, ntis** *c*
back   **tergum, i** *n*
bad   **malus, a, um**
bailiff   **uilicus, i** *m*
bake   **coquo, ere, xi, ctum**
bandit   **latro, onis** *m*
banker   **argentarius, ii** *m*
barbarian   **barbarus, i** *m*

bark   **latro** [1]
basket   **corbis, is** *m/f*
baths   **thermae, arum** *f pl*
battle   **pugna, ae** *f*; **proelium, ii** *n*; (campaign) **bellum, i** *n*
battlefield   **locus pugnae**
beast   **fera, ae** *f*
beat   (~ up) **uerbero** [1]; (conquer) **supero** [1]; †**uinco**
beautiful   **pulcher, chra, chrum**
beauty   **pulchritudo, inis** *f*
because   *see pp. 99–100*
because of   **propter**; **ob** *both* + *acc*
become   †**fio**
bed   **lectus, i** *m*
bedroom   **cubiculum, i** *n*
bedtime   **hora somni**
bee   **apis, is** *f*
before *p*   **ante** + *acc*
before *adv*   **antea**; **antehac**; *see pp. 81–2*
beg   **oro** [1]
begin   †**in-cipio**; **coepi, isse** *in past tense only*
behalf: on ~ of   **pro** + *abl*
behave   **me** †**gero**
behind   **post** + *acc*
behold *int*   **ecce**
believe   †**credo** + *dat*
below   **sub** + *abl*; **infra** + *acc*
benefit   †**pro-sum** + *dat*
bereaved   **orbatus, a, um**
besides   **praeterea**
best   **optimus, a, um**
between   **inter** + *acc*
beyond   **ultra** + *acc*; go ~ (fig.) **antecello, ere** + *dat*
bidding   **iussus, us** *m*; at my ~ **meo iussu**
bide   *see* stay
big: so ~   **tantus, a, um**
bind   †**uincio**
bird   **auis, is** *f*
birthday   **dies natalis** *f*
bitter   **acerbus, a, um**
blame   **culpo** [1]
blue   **caeruleus, a, um**
blush   **erubesco, ere, bui**
board   †**con-scendo**
boast   **glorior** [1]

boat   **nauicula, ae** *f*
body   **corpus, oris** *n*
bodyguard   **satellites, um** *m pl*
boil   **coquo, ere, coxi, coctum**
boldness   **audacia, ae** *f*
bone   **os, ossis** *n*
book   **liber, bri** *m*
booty   **praeda, ae** *f*
bore   (cause tedium) **fatigo** [1]
boring   **molestus, a, um**
born   **natus, a, um**
borrow   **mutuor** [1]
both   (together) **ambo, ae**; (individually) **uterque, traque, trumque**; ~ ... and ... **et ... et ...**; **cum ... tum ...**
boulder   **saxum, i** *n*
bound: be ~ to   *see p. 120*
bow   (weapon) **arcus, us** *m*
boy   **puer, eri** *m*
boyfriend   **amicus, i** *m*
branch   **ramus, i** *m*
brave   **fortis, e**
bread   **panis, is** *m*
break   (into pieces) †**frango**; (~ faith) **uiolo** [1]
breed   (tend) †**colo**
bridge   **pons, pontis** *m*
bring   †**ad-fero**; †**duco**; ~ forth (give birth) **gigno, ere, genui, genitum**; (found) **condo, ere, didi, ditum**; ~ out †**pro-duco**
brooch   **fibula, ae** *f*
brothel   **lupanar, ris** *n*
brother   **frater, tris** *m*
brown   (tawny) **fuluus, a, um**
build   **aedifico** [1]
building   **aedificium, ii** *n*
bull   **taurus, i** *m*
burn *vi*   **ardeo, ere, si**
bury   †**sepelio**
business   **res, rerum** *f pl*
but   **sed**; **autem**; **at**
buy   †**emo**
buyer   **emptor, is** *m*
by   (of agent) **a(b)** + *abl*; (near) **prope** + *acc*

cage   **saeptum, i** *n*
cake   **placenta, ae** *f*

call   **uoco** [1]; ~ for †**arcesso**; ~ together **conuoco** [1]; ~ by name **nomino** [1]
calmly   **aequo animo**
camp   **castra, orum** *n pl*
can   (I am able) **possum, posse, potui**
captain   **dux, ducis** *m*
capture   †**capio**
care *v*   **interest** + *dat of person caring*; ~ for **curo** [1]
care: without a ~ **securus, a, um**; take ~ of **curo** [1]; take ~ that **curo** [1] **ut** + *subj*; take ~ that ... not **caueo, ere, caui, cautum ne** + *subj*
careful   **diligens** (*gen* ntis)
carry   **porto** [1]; †**fero**; ~ out (effect) †**ef-ficio**; (perform) †**fungor** + *abl*
case   (in court) **causa, ae** *f*, **res, rei** *f*, **actio, onis** *f*; in ~ **ne** + *subj*; **si forte** + *subj*
cat   **feles, is** *f*
catch   †**capio**
cattle   **boues, boum** *m/f pl*
cave   **spelunca, ae** *f*
cease   †**de-sino**
centurion   **centurio, onis** *m*
century   **saeculum, i** *n*
certain   (sure) **certus, a, um**; (a ~) **quidam, quaedam, quoddam**
certainly   **certe**; **quidem**
chain   **uinculum, i** *n*
chair   **sedes, is** *f*, **sella, ae** *f*
change   **muto** [1]
character   **ingenium, ii** *n*
charge   (with crime) **accuso** [1]
charge: be in ~ of   †**prae-sum** + *dat*
chariot   **currus, us** *m*
charming   **amoenus, a, um**
chase   †**per-sequor**
cheese   **caseus, i** *m*
chest   **pectus, oris** *n*
chicken   **pullus, i** *m*
chief, chieftain   **princeps, ipis** *m*
children   **liberi, orum** *m pl*
choice: have a ~ **diiudicare possum, posse, potui**; make a ~ **diiudico** [1]
choose   (select) **eligo, ere, legi, lectum**; (decide) †**con-stituo**
circumstances   **res, rerum** *f pl*

citizen **ciuis, is** *m*

city **urbs, is** *f*

civil war **bellum ciuile** *n*

clever **callidus, a, um**

client **cliens, ntis** *m*

climb †**a-scendo**; ~ over †**tran-scendo**

cloak **pallium, ii** *n*

clothes **uestis, is** *f*; **uestimenta, orum** *n pl*

cloud **nubes, is** *f*

collapse **labor, i, psus sum**

colour **color, is** *m*

come †**uenio**; ~ out †**ex-eo**; ~ to †**ad-uenio**; (fig.) *see* begin

comedy **comoedia, ae** *f*

comfort *v* **consolor** [1]

comfort *n* **solacium, ii** *n*

command *v* †**iubeo**; **impero** [1] + *dat*

command *n* **imperium, ii** *n*; at my ~ **meo iussu**

comment **rumor, is** *m*

commit †**com-mitto**

common **uulgaris, e**; ~ people **plebeii, orum** *m pl*

community **respublica, reipublicae** *f*

companion **socius, ii** *m*

compare †**con-fero** (to + *dat*)

compete **certo** [1]

complain †**queror**

complete **integer, gra, grum**

completely **omnino**

conceal **celo** [1]

condemn **damno** [1]

congratulate **gratulor** [1] + *dat*

conquer **supero** [1]

conscript †**con-scribo**

consecrate **consecro** [1]

consider (someone something) **habeo** [2]; †**duco**

console **solacio** ǀ**sum** + *dat*; (con)**solor** [1]

conspirator **coniuratus, i** *m*

consul **consul, is** *m*

consult †**consulo**; ~ the interests of †**consulo** + *dat*

contemptible: be ~ **ludibrio** †**sum**

content **contentus, a, um**

convict **damno** [1]

cook *n* **coquus, i** *m*

cook *v* **coquo, ere, coxi, coctum**

corrupt †**cor-rumpo**

corruption **deprauatio, onis** *f*

count **numero** [1]

country *n* (land) **terra, ae** *f*; (countryside) **rus, ruris** *n*

country *a* **rusticus, a, um**; ~ estate **uilla, ae** *f*

courage **fortitudo, inis** *f*; **uirtus, utis** *f*

courtyard **area, ae** *f*

cover **celo** [1]

cowardly **ignauus, a, um**

craftsman **faber, bri** *m*

create **creo** [1]

creep out †**e-gredior**

crime **delictum, i** *n*

crimson **coccinus, a, um**

crow **cornix, cis** *f*

crown *n* **corona, ae** *f*

crown *v* **corono** [1]

crucial **maximi momenti** (*gen*)

crucify **cruci suffigo, ere, ixi, ixum**

cruel **crudelis, e**

cry (of baby) **uagio** [4]; (weep) **lacrimo** [1]; ~ out **exclamo** [1]

cue **signum, i** *n*

cunning **callidus, a, um**

cup **poculum, i** *n*

cure **medicamentum, i** *n*

curious = 'wanting to know'

curse **uitupero** [1]

cut †**seco**; (~ to pieces) **trucido** [1]; ~ off **praecido, ere, idi, isum**

dagger **pugio, onis** *m*

daily **cotidie**

dance **salto** [1]

danger **periculum, i** *n*; be in ~ **periclitor** [1]

dangerous **periculosus, a, um**

dark **tenebricosus, a, um**; it grows ~ **uesperascit**

darkness **tenebrae, arum** *f pl*

daughter **filia, ae** *f*

dawn **solis ortus, us** *m*

day **dies, ei** *m/f*; one ~ (once) **olim**

deaf **surdus, a, um**

dear   carus, a, um
death   mors, mortis *f*
debtor   debitor, is *m*
decadence   luxuria, ae *f*; stuprum, i *n*
deceitful   fallax (gen acis)
deceive   †fallo
decide   †constituo (to + *infin*)
declare   pronuntio [1]
decree   †de-cerno
dedicate   dedico [1]
deep   altus, a, um
deeply: be ~ in love with   *see* devoted
defeat   †uinco
defend   defendo, ere, di
defendant   reus, i *m*
delay   moror [1]; cunctor [1]
delicate   (texture) subtilis, e
delighted: be ~   †gaudeo
delightful   lepidus, a, um
demand   postulo [1]
deny   nego [1], *see pp. 61, 119–21*
depict   *see* paint
deserve   mereor [2]
despair   despero [1]
desperation   desperatio, onis *f*
despise   contemno, ere, mpsi, mptum
destroy   †deleo; †e-uerto
destruction   pernicies, ei *f*
devise   (a plan) †capio
devote   dedo, ere, dedidi deditum; ~
   oneself to studeo [2] + *dat*
devoted: be ~ to   (love) amo [1]
devotion   studium, ii *n*
die   †morior
different   *see p. 54*
difficult   difficilis, e
dig   †fodio
dignity   dignitas, atis *f*
diligently   diligenter
dining room   triclinium, ii *n*
dinner   cena, ae *f*
directions   partes, ium *f pl*
disappear   euanesco, ere, nui
disaster   clades, is *f*
discover   (find out) †cognosco; (come
   across) comperio [4]; †in-uenio
discus   discus, i *m*

discuss   dissero, ere, serui, sertum de +
   abl
disease   pestilentia, ae *f*
disguise oneself   uestem muto [1]
dishonesty   fraus, fraudis *f*
dishonour   turpitudo, inis *f*; ignominia,
   ae *f*
dislike   = 'not like'; *see also* hate
disrespect   impietas, atis *f*; insolentia, ae
   f
distance: be at a ~   †ab-sum
distress   ango, ere, nxi, nctum
disturb   sollicito [1]
ditch   fossa, ae *f*
divert   †a-uerto
divide   diuido, ere, isi, isum
do   †facio; †ago; don't ...! noli, nolite +
   infin; *see also p. 68*
doctor   medicus, i *m*
dog   canis, is *m*
door   ianua, ae *f*
doubt   dubito [1]
down: go ~   †de-scendo
drag   †traho
draw up   (document) †scribo; (line of
   battle) †in-struo
dreadful   terribilis, e
dream   somnium, ii *n*
drink *n*   potus, us *m*
drink *v*   †bibo
drive: ~ away repello, ere, reppuli,
   repulsum; ~ out expello, ere, expuli,
   expulsum
drought   siccitas, atis *f*
dry *a*   siccus, a, um
dry *v*   abstergo, ere, rsi
during   inter + *acc*
dust   puluis, eris *m*
duty   officium, ii *n*
dwarf   pumilio, onis *m*

each   quisque; *see also pp. 55–6, 157*; ~
   other *see p. 56*
eager   cupidus, a, um; studiosus, a, um
eagerness   studium, ii *n*
eagle   aquila, ae *f*
ear   auris, is *f*

early (in the morning) **mane**; (timely) **mature**

earnestly **impense**; **intente**

earth (world) **orbis terrarum** *m*

earthquake **terrae tremores, um** *m pl*

ease **leuo** [1]; **mollio** [4]

easy **facilis, e**

eat †**edo** (*pl impv* **este**)

edge **finis, is** *m*

effort **labor, is** *m*

egg **ouum, i** *n*

eight **octo**

either ... or *see p. 128*

elephant **elephantus, i** *m*

eleventh **undecimus, a, um**

elder **natu maior**

eloquent **facundus, a, um**

embrace †**amplector**

emperor **princeps, ipis** *m*

empty **inanis, e; uacuus, a, um**

encourage **hortor** [1]

end *n* **finis, is** *m*; in the ~ *see* finally

end *vi* **finior** [4]

endearing **carus, a, um; uenustus, a, um**

endow **dono** [1] + *acc of person, abl of thing*

endowed **praeditus, a, um** (with + *abl*)

endure **diu** †**super-sum**

enemy (military) **hostes, ium** *m pl*; (private) **inimicus, i** *m*

enjoy †**fruor** + *abl*; *see also* please, like

enough **satis** + *gen*; be ~ †**satis-facio** + *dat*

enraged **iratus, a, um**

enter **intro** [1]

entice **elicio, ere, cui**

entirely **omnino**

entrance **aditus, us** *m*

entrust **dedo, ere, dedidi, deditum**

equal **aequalis, e**

escape †**ef-fugio**

especially (above all) **praesertim; praecipue**; (extremely) **ualde**

even **etiam**

evening: in the ~ **uesperi**

eventually *see* finally

ever after **in aeternum**

every: ~ day **cotidie**; ~ year **quotannis**

everyone **omnes, ium** *m pl*

everywhere **ubique**

evidence **testimonium, ii** *n*; **indicium, ii** *n*

exam **examinatio, onis** *f*

examine †**in-spicio**

example **exemplar, is** *n*; **exemplum, i** *n*

excellent **optimus, a, um; egregius, a, um**

except **praeter** + *acc*; **nisi**

exclaim **clamo** [1]

exclude **excludo, ere, usi, usum**

exercise **exerceo** [2]

execute (kill) †**inter-ficio**

exhaust (tire out) **fatigo** [1]

exile **relego** [1]

exist †**sum**; not ~ **nusquam** †**sum**

expect **exspecto** [1]

experienced **peritus, a, um** (in + *gen*)

explain †**ex-pono**

express **exprimo, ere, essi, essum**

extremely *see* very

eye **oculus, i** *m*

face (human) **uultus, us** *m*; (surface) **facies, ei** *f*

fail †**de-ficio; concido, ere, di**

failure (lack) **defectio, onis** *f*; (fault) **delictum, i** *n*

fair (pretty) **formosus, a, um**; (light coloured) **flauus, a, um**; (just) **iustus, a, um**; (weather) **serenus, a, um**

faith **fides, ei** *f*

faithful **fidelis, e**

fall *n* **casus, us** *m*

fall *v* †**cado; excido, ere, di**

fame **fama, ae** *f*

family (household) **familia, ae** *f*; (clan) **gens, gentis** *f*

famous **clarus, a, um; notus, a, um**

fancy †**cupio**

far: as ~ as **tenus** + *abl or gen*; ~ off *adv* **procul**

farewell **uale**

farm **fundus, i** *m*

farmer **agricola, ae**

fast **celer, eris, ere**

father **pater, tris** *m*

fatherland **patria, ae** *f*

fault   **culpo** [1]

favour *v*   †**faueo** + *dat*

favour *n*: be in someone's ~   †**pro-sum** + *dat*

fear *n*   **metus, us** *m*

fear *v*   **timeo** [2]; †**metuo; uereor** [2]

feel   (handle) **tracto** [1]; (emotion) †**sentio**

few   **pauci, ae, a**

field   **ager, gri** *m*

fifteen   **quindecim**

fifth   **quintus, a, um**

fight   **pugno** [1]

files   **tabulae, arum** *f pl*

finally   **postremo; tandem; denique**

find   †**in-uenio; reperio, ire, repperi, rtum;** ~ out †**cognosco**

fine   **bonus, a, um**

finger   **digitus, i** *m*

finish *vt*   †**con-ficio; finio** [4]; *vi* **finior** [4]

finishing line   **meta, ae** *f*

fire   **ignis, is** *m*; **incendium, i** *n*

first *a*   **primus, a, um**

first *adv*   **primum; primo**

fish   **piscis, is** *m*

fitting: it is ~   **decet** + *acc*

flatter   **blandior** [4] + *dat*

flee   †**fugio;** †**con-fugio**

fleet   **classis, is** *f*

flight   (escape) **fuga, ae** *f*; (of birds) **uolatus, us** *m*

float   **innato** [1]

flock   **grex, gis** *m*

flogging   *use* **uerbera, um** *n pl*

flood   **inundo** [1]

flow   **fluo, ere, xi, ctum**

flower   **flos, floris** *m*

flute player   **tibicen, inis** *m*; **tibicina, ae** *f*

fly *v*   **uolo** [1]

fly *m*   **musca, ae** *f*

foliage   **folia, orum** *n pl*

follow   †**sequor**

fond of   **cupidus, a, um** + *gen*

food   **cibus, i** *m*; **alimentum, i** *n*

foolish   **stultus, a, um**

foot   **pes, dis** *m*

for *p*   (on behalf of) **pro** + *abl*; (to benefit) *use dat*; (of time) *use acc*

for *c*   **enim; nam;** *see pp. 126–7*

forbid   †**ueto**

force   **cogo, ere, coegi, coactum**

foreman   **uilicus, i** *m*

forest   **silua, ae** *f*

forget   †**obliuiscor** + *gen*

forgive   †**ignosco** + *dat*

former: the ~   **ille, a, ud**

fort   **castellum, i** *n*

fortune   **fortuna, ae** *f*

forty   **quadraginta**

forum   **forum, i** *n*

four   **quattuor;** ~ times *a* **quadruplex** (*gen* **icis**); *adv* **quater**

fox   **uulpes, is** *f*

free   **liber, era, erum**

free: set ~   **libero** [1]

freedman   **libertus, i** *m*

frequently   **saepe**

friend   **amicus, i** *m*; **amica, ae** *f*

friendly   **comis, e**

fright   **metus, us** *m*

frightened: be ~ *see* fear; thoroughly ~ **perterritus, a, um**

frightful   **terribilis, e; horribilis, e; formidolosus, a, um**

front: in ~ of   **ante** + *acc*

fugitive   **fugitiuus, a, um**

full   **plenus, a, um** + *gen*

future: in (the) ~   **in posterum**

gambol   **lasciuio** [4]

game   **ludus, i** *m*

garden   **hortum, i** *n*

garland   **corona, ae** *f*

gate   **porta, ae** *f*

gather   †**lego**

general   **imperator, is** *m*

generation   **stirps, is** *f*

genius   **ingenium, ii** *n*

get   †**ac-cipio; nanciscor, i, na(n)ctus sum;** ~ up †**surgo;** ~ in **intro** [1]

ghost   **umbra, ae** *f*

girl   **puella, ae** *f*

girlfriend   **amica, ae** *f*

give   †**do;** ~ up **dedo, ere, dedidi, deditum**

glad: be ~   †**gaudeo**

gladiator   **gladiator, is** *m*
glass merchant   **uitrearius, ii** *m*
glitter   **mico, are, cui**
go   †**eo**; ~ forward †**pro-gredior**; ~ away
  †**ab-eo**; ~ out †**ex-eo**; ~ past †**praetereo**;
  ~ across †**trans-eo**; ~ down †**de-scendo**
god   **deus, i** *m*
goddess   **dea, ae** *f*
gold *n*   **aurum, i** *n*
gold *a*, golden   **aureus, a, um**; ~ piece
  aureus, i *m*
good   **bonus, a, um**
goose   **anser, is** *m*
govern   †**rego**
governor   **praefectus, i** *m*
grab   †**rapio**
graceful   **decorus, a, um**
grammar   **grammatica, ae** *f*
grandfather   **auus, i** *m*
graze   **pascor, i, pastus sum**
great   **magnus, a, um**
green   **uiridis, e**
greet   **saluto** [1]
grief   **dolor, is** *m*
grieve   **doleo** [2]
ground   **humus, i** *f*; **terra, ae** *f*
group   **caterua, ae** *f*
grow angry, dark, etc. *see* angry, dark, etc.;
  see also become
grunt   **grunnio** [4]
guard *n*   **custos, odis** *m*
guard *v*   **custodio** [4]
guest   **hospes, itis** *m*

habits   **mores, morum** *m pl*
hair   **capilli, orum** *m pl*
hand   **manus, us** *f*; ~ to ~ **comminus**
hand over   **trado, dere, didi, ditum**
happen   †**fio**; **accido, ere, idi**; †**e-uenio**
happiness   **felicitas, atis** *f*
happy   **felix** (*gen* **icis**)
harbour   **portus, us** *m*
hard *adv*   (industriously) **diligenter**
hard work   **diligentia, ae** *f*
hardly   **uix; aegre**
harm   **laedo, ere, si, sum**
harvest: reap the ~   **meto, ere, messui,
  messum**

hate   **odi, isse**
have   (possess) **habeo** [2]; (enjoy) †**fruor**
  + *abl*; ~ to (must) **debeo** [2]
head   **caput, itis** *n*; keep one's ~ **aequo
  animo** †**sum** *or* me †**gero**
health   **salus, utis** *f*
hear   **audio** [4]
heat   **aestus, us** *m*
helmsman   **gubernator, is** *m*
help *n*   **auxilium, ii** *n*
help *v*   †**ad-iuuo**
herald   **praeco, onis** *m*
here   **hic**; ~ and now **ilico**
hero   **heros, ois** *m* (*acc* **oem**)
hesitate   **dubito** [1]
hide *vt*   **celo** [1]
high   **altus, a, um**
hill   **collis, is** *m*; **mons, montis** *m*
hinder   †**ob-sto** + *dat*; **impedio** [4]
hire   †**con-duco**
hold   **teneo** [2]
hole   **foramen, inis** *n*; **rima, ae** *f*
honest   **probus, a, um**
honesty   **honestas, atis** *f*; **probitas, atis** *f*
honey   **mel, mellis** *n*
honour *n*   **honos, oris** *m*; **decus, oris** *n*
honour *v*   **celebro** [1]
hope *v*   **spero** [1]
horrible   (nasty) **malignus, a, um**
horrified: be ~   **commoueor, eri, otus
  sum**
horror   **horror, is** *m*
horse   **equus, i** *m*
hostage   **obses, idis** *m*
hour   **hora, ae** *f*
house   **domus, us** *f*; **aedes, ium** *f pl*;
  (hovel) **casa, ae** *f*
how   (in what way) **quo modo**
however   (but) **tamen**; (to whatever
  extent) **quamuis** *see pp. 100–1*
howl   **ululo** [1]
huge   **ingens** (*gen* **ntis**)
human being   **homo, inis** *m*
hungry: be ~   **esurio** [4]
hunt   **uenor** [1]
hurry   **festino** [1]; **propero** [1]
hurt   **laedo, ere, si, sum**
husband   **maritus, i** *m*; **uir, uiri** *m*

hut   **casa, ae** *f*

I   **ego**; I personally **equidem**
idiot   **stultus, a, um**
idle   **ignauus, a, um**
if   **si**; ~ … not **nisi**
ill *a*   **aeger, gra, grum**; fall ~ **aegroto** [1]
ill *adv*   (badly) **malum**
immoral   **impudicus, a, um**
importance   **momentum, i** *n*
important   **grauis, e**
improper thing   **dedecus, oris** *n*
improve *vi*   **melior** †**fio**
inalienable   **qui abalienari non potest**
increase   **augeo, ere, xi, ctum**
indeed   (but/and in fact) **uero**
inflame   **inflammo** [1]
inhabitant   **incola, ae** *m*
injustice   **iniuria, ae** *f*
innkeeper   **caupo, onis** *m*
inside   **intro**; **intus**; *see p. 18*
inspect   †**in-spicio**
inspire   †**ad-duco**
instead   (rather) **potius**
instigator   **auctor, is** *m*
instruction   **praeceptum, i** *n*
insult   **obiurgo** [1]
interest   (attention) **studium, ii** *n*
interested   **studiosus, a, um**; **attentus, a, um**
into   **in** + *acc*
invade   **inuado, ere asi, asum in** + *acc*; †**in-curro**
invent   **excogito** [1]; †**fingo**
investigate   **inquiro, ere, isiui, isitum**; **inuestigo** [1]
invite   **inuito** [1]
island   **insula, ae** *f*

jewellery   **ornamenta, orum** *n pl*; **gemmae, arum** *f pl*
jewels   **gemmae, arum** *f pl*
job   **opus, eris** *n*
join   †**iungo**
journey   **iter, itineris** *n*
joy   **gaudium, ii** *n*
judge *m*   **iudex, icis** *m*
judge *v*   **iudico** [1]
jump   †**salio**

keep   **retineo** [2]; ~ on doing *use adv* **saepius**
key   **clauis, is** *f*
kill   †**inter-ficio**; **neco, are, c(a)ui, atum**; ~ …self **mortem mihi conscisco, ere, iui, itum**
kind: of this ~   **huiusmodi** *indecl*
kindness   **beneficium, ii** *n*
king   **rex, regis** *m*
kingdom   **regnum, i** *n*
kitchen   **culina, ae** *f*
knife   **culter, tri** *m*
know   **scio** [4] (how to + *infin*); (be acquainted with) **noui, isse**; not ~ **nescio** [4]

labour   **laboro** [1]
lack   **careo** [2] + *abl*
lake   **lacus, us** *m*
lamb   **agnus, i** *m*
lamp   **lucerna, ae** *f*
language   **lingua, ae** *f*
large   **grandis, e**; **magnus, a, um**
last   (furthest) **ultimus, a, um**; (final) **postremus, a, um**; (previous) **superior, ius**; **prior, ius**; at ~ *see* finally
late   (at night) **multa nocte**; (too ~) **serius**
later   **postea**; **posthac**
Latin (language)   **lingua Latina** *f*
latter: the ~   **hic, haec, hoc**
laugh   †**rideo**
laurel   **laureus, a, um**
law   **lex, legis** *f*
lay   (egg) †**pario**; (a trap) **paro** [1]; ~ aside †**de-pono**
lead   †**duco**
leader   **dux, ducis** *m*
leafy   **frondosus, a, um**
lean against   **innitor, i, ixus sum** + *dat*
leap   *see* jump
learn   †**disco**
least: at ~   **saltem**
leave   †**relinquo**
lecture   *use* **schola, ae** *f*
ledge   **promuntorium, ii** *n*
legion   **legio, onis** *f*
lend   (money) **commodo** [1]

lengths: go to great ~   omnia tento [1]
less   minus
letter   litterae, arum *f pl*; epistula, ae *f*
liberty   libertas, atis *f*
library   bibliotheca, ae *f*
lick   demulceo, ere, lsi
lie *n*   falsum, i *n*
lie[1] *vi*   (tell untruth) mentior [4]; falsa †dico
lie[2] *vi*   (~ down) iaceo [2]
life   uita, ae *f*
lift   †tollo
light *n*   lumen, inis *n*
light *v*   (ignite) accendo, ere, ndi, nsum
like *v*   amo [1]; *see also* please
like *a*   similis, e + *gen*
limb   membrum, i *n*
line   (battle~) acies, ei *f*
linger   *see* stay
lion   leo, onis *m*
listen   *see* hear
lithe   mollis, e
litter   (sedan chair) lectica, ae *f*
little   paruus, a, um; so ~ tantulus, a, um
live   †uiuo; (dwell) habito [1]
loan   pecunia mutua *f*
lobster   locusta, ae *f*
local   finitimus, a, um
lock   obsero [1]
long: for a ~ time diu; ~ ago iamdudum
longer   diutius; no ~ non iam
look   (watch, ~ at) specto [1]; ~ after curo [1]; ~ upon as habeo [2]
lose   †a-mitto
lost: get ~   aberro [1]
loud   clarus, a, um
love *n*   amor, is *m*
love *v*   amo [1]
lover   amator, is *m*; amatrix, icis *f*
loyalty   fidelitas, atis *f*
lucky   felix (*gen* icis); fortunatus, a, um
luxurious   luxuriosus, a, um; sumptuosus, a, um

magnificent   splendidus, a, um
maid(servant)   ancilla, ae *f*
maiden   uirgo, ginis *f*

make   (create, cause) †facio; ~ for †peto; ~ love (to) amo [1]; ~ one's way *see* go; ~ merry commissor [1]; ~ progress bene †pro-ficio
man   (human being) homo, inis *m*; (as opposed to woman) uir, i *m*
manager   uilicus, i *m*
mansion   domus, us *f*
many   multi, ae, a; as/so ~ tot *indec*
marble   marmoreus, a, um
marketplace   forum, i *n*
marriage   matrimonium, ii *n*
marry   (of woman) †nubo + *dat of man*; (of man) uxorem †duco
master   dominus, i *m*; (school~) magister, tri *m*
match: be no ~ for   impar †sum + *dat*
matron   matrona, ae *f*
matter   res, rei *f*
meadow   pratum, i *n*
meal   cena, ae *f*
meat   caro, carnis *f*
meet   (go to ~, encounter) †oc-curro + *dat*; (come together) †con-uenio
merchant   mercator, is *m*
merely   (in fact only) immo
messenger   nuntius, ii *m*
midday   meridies, ei *m*
mile   mille passus, uum *m pl; see p. 155–6*
military qualities   disciplina militaris *f*
milk   lac, ctis *n*
miracle   portentum, i *n*
mistake: make a ~   erro [1]
misuse   †ab-utor + *abl*
mob   turba, ae *f*
mock   †ir-rideo
money   pecunia, ae *f*
monster   monstrum, i *n*
month   mensis, is *m*
moon   luna, ae *f*
more   (of quantity) plus + *gen*; (of degree) magis
morning: in the ~   mane
mortal   mortalis, e
moss   muscus, i *m*
most   maxima pars *f*; plurimi, ae, a *pl*
mother   mater, tris *f*
motive   ratio, onis *f*

mountain **mons, montis** *m*; ~ pass **iugum, i** *n*
mourn **gemo, ere, ui, itum**
mouth **os, oris** *n*
move *vt* †**moueo**
much **multus, a, um**
mug (beat up) **pulso** [1]
mugger **latro, onis** *m*
mule **mulus, i** *m*
murder **caedes, is** *f*
murderer **sicarius, ii** *m*
music **carmina, um** *n pl*
must (have to) **debeo** [1]
my **meus, a, um**
mystery **mysterium, ii** *n*

naked **nudus, a, um**
name *v* **nomino** [1]
name *n* **nomen, inis** *n*; by the ~ of **nomine** *invar*
nasty **molestus, a, um**
nation **populus, i** *m*
nature **natura, ae** *f*
naughty **improbus, a, um**
near **prope** + *acc*
nearest **proximus, a, um**
neck **ceruix, icis** *f*
need **opus est** + *dat of person, abl of thing needed*; **egeo** [2] + *abl*
neglect †**neg-lego**
neighbouring **finitimus, a, um**
never **numquam**
nevertheless **nihilominus**
new **nouus, a, um**
news **nuntium, ii** *n* (of + *gen*)
next **insequens** (*gen* ntis); on the ~ day **postridie**
nice (pleasant) **suauis, e**
nick: in the ~ of time **peropportune**
night **nox, noctis** *f*
nightfall: at *or* by **sub noctem**
nimble **agilis, e**
nine **nouem**
nineteen **undeuiginti** *indecl*
ninth **nonus, a, um**
no **nullus, a, um**
nobody, no one **nemo, nullius**
noble **nobilis, e**

nor *see pp. 127–8*
nose **nasus, i** *m*
not **non; haud**; and … ~ **nec; neque**; ~ at all **haudquaquam; nullo modo**; ~ only … but also *see p. 127*; not even **ne … quidem**
note *n* **litterae, arum** *f pl*; of ~ **notabilis, e; monstrabilis, e**
note *v* *see* notice
nothing **nihil** *n*
notice **animaduerto, ere, i**
now **nunc; iam**
nowadays **hodie**
nowhere **nusquam**
nurse **nutrix, cis** *f*

obey **pareo** [2] + *dat*
obtain **nanciscor, i, nactus sum**
occasionally **interdum**
occur: it ~s to me **mihi uenit in mentem**
offend **offendo, ere, di, nsum**
offer **offero, offerre, obtuli, oblatum**
office (duty) **officium, ii** *n*; (room) **tabularium, ii** *n*; **tablinum, i** *n*
often **saepe**
oil **oleum, i** *n*
old (of things) **antiquus, a, um**; ~ man **senex, is** *m*; ~ woman **anus, us** *f*; ~ soldier **ueteranus, i** *m*
once *adv* (on some occasion) **olim**; (on a single occasion) **semel**
one **unus, a, um**; ~ at a time **singuli, ae, a** *pl*; *see p. 157*
only **solum**
open †**aperio**
opinion **sententia, ae** *f*
oracle (prophecy) **oraculum, i** *n*; ~ at Delphi (priestess) **Pythia, ae** *f*
orator **orator, is** *m*
order **impero** [1] + *dat*; †**iubeo**
other *see pp. 53–4*; each ~ *see p. 56*
ought **debeo** [2] + *infin*
our **noster, tra, trum**
out of **ex** + *abl*
outside **foris; foras**; *see p. 18*
outstanding **egregius, a, um**
overboard **in mare**
overcome *vt* **supero** [1]

overcome *a* confectus, a, um
overrun peruagor [1]
overtake †as-sequor
overwhelm obruo, ere, ui, utum
own proprius, a, um

pain dolor, is *m*; cause ~ doleo + *dat*
paint pingo, ere, nxi, pictum
painter pictor, is *m*
painting pictura, ae *f*
palace regia, ae *f*
pallid pallidus, a, um
panic-stricken perterritus, a, um
pant anhelo [1]
pardon ignosco, ere, oui, otum + *dat*; *see
    also* spare
parent genitor, is *c*; parens, ntis *c*
part *n* pars, partis *f*; the ~ of *use gen, see
    p. 8*
part *vt* separo [1]
party (gathering) conuiuium, ii *n*
patron patronus, i *m*
pay (taxes) pendo, ere, pependi, pensum
peace pax, cis *f*
peaceful tranquillus, a, um
pearl margarita, ae *f*; gemma, ae *f*
peasant agrestis, is *m*
peep per rimam speculor [1]
penalty: pay the ~ poenas †do
people (a nation) populus, i *m*; (an
    unspecified group) *use impersonal passive,
    see pp. 77–8; see also* man
perform (carry out) fungor, i, nctus sum
    + *abl*; (put on entertainment)
    spectaculum edo, ere, didi, ditum
perhaps fortasse; (as chance would have
    it) forsitan + *subj*
perish †per-eo
permitted: it is ~ licet + *dat*
personally: I ~ equidem
persuade †suadeo + *dat*
pet permulceo, ere, lsi
phial ampulla, ae *f*
philosopher philosophus, i *m*
philosophy philosophia, ae *f*
pick (pluck) †carpo; ~ up †tollo; †sumo
piece (coin): ~ of silver argenteus, i *m*; ~
    of gold aureus, i *m*

pilgrim peregrinus, i *m*
pink roseus, a, um
pirate praedo, onis *m*
pit fouea, ae *f*
pitch (camp) †pono
pity miseret + *acc of person pitying, gen of
    person/thing pitied*
place †de-pono
plague pestis, is *f*
plain (flat ground) campus, i *m*
plan *n* (plot) consilium, ii *n*; (blueprint)
    descriptio, onis *f*
plan *v* (plot) consilium †capio; (contrive)
    †struo
play *n* comoedia, ae *f*; tragoedia, ae *f*
play *v* (game) †ludo; (music) †cano
plead (a case) causam †ago
pleasant amoenus, a, um
please *v* placeo [2] + *dat*; delecto [1]
pleasure uoluptas, atis *f*
plot coniuratio, onis *f*
plough aro [1]
poem carmen, inis *n*
poet poeta, ae *m*
poetry *see* poems, verses
poison uenenum, i *n*
politician uir rerum politicarum peritus
    m
poor pauper (*gen* ris)
pop (~ music) carmina popularia *n pl*
port portus, i *m*
portion pars, rtis *f*
possible: as … as ~ quam + *sup*
pound libra, ae *f*
pour †fundo
power imperium, ii *n*; potestas, atis *f*
powerful potens (*gen* ntis)
praise *v* laudo [1]
praise *n* laus, dis *f*
praiseworthy laudabilis, e
pray precor [1]; adoro [1]; ~ to supplico
    [1] + *dat*
prefer malo, malle, malui
prepare paro [1]
presence: in the ~ of coram + *abl*
present *n* donum, i *n*
present *a*: be ~ (at) †ad-sum (+ *dat*)
preserve conseruo [1]

pretend simulo [1]
pretty pulcher, chra, chrum
prevent prohibeo [2], *see p. 121*; to ~ (so that ... not) ne + *subj, see pp. 86–7*
previous prior, ius; superior, ius; on the ~ day pridie
price pretium, ii *n; see also pp. 8, 11*
priest sacerdos, otis *m*
prince princeps, cipis *m*
prison carcer, ris *m*
prisoner captiuus, i *m*
prize praemium, ii *n*
procession pompa, ae *f*
promise polliceor [2]
properly rite
propose †suadeo + *acc of thing proposed*
proscribe †pro-scribo
proud superbus, a, um (of + *abl*)
prove demonstro [1]
provide better evidence = 'be more to be trusted'
province prouincia, ae *f*
pub taberna, ae *f*
publish edo, ere, edidi, editum
punish punio [4]
pupil discipulus, i *m*
purple purpureus, a, um
pursuit studium, ii *n*
put †pono; ~ down †de-pono; ~ on induo, ere, ui, utum; ~ in †im-pono; insero, ere, rui, rtum

quality uirtus, utis *f*
queen regina, ae *f*
quick *see* fast
quickly (fast) celeriter; (soon) cito
quietly cum silentio
quite (very) ualde; admodum; prorsus; (to a limited degree) satis; ita + *result clause*

rabbit cuniculus, i *m*
race cursus, us *m*
rain imber, bris *m*
rain *v*: it ~s pluit
rather than potius ... quam
razor nouacula, ae *f*
reach (come to) †per-uenio, †ad-uenio ad + *acc*

read †lego
ready paratus, a, um
realise comprehendo, ere, di, nsum
really ualde
realm regnum, i *n*
reap the harvest meto, ere, messui, messum
reasonable aequus, a, um; iustus, a, um
recall reuoco [1]
receive †ac-cipio
recently nuper
recitation recitatio, onis *f*
recognise †cognosco
recover conualesco, ere, ui
referee arbiter, tri *m*
refrain = 'hinder oneself'
refugee exsul, is *c*
refuse recuso [1]; nolo *ir*
regain recipero [1]
regret paenitet + *acc of person feeling regret, gen of thing regretted*
regular (daily) cotidianus, a, um
reign regno [1]
reject reicio, ere, ieci, iectum
rejoice †gaudeo
relent mitigor [1]
relieve leuo [1]
remaining reliquus, a, um
remarkable insignis, e; mirus, a, um
remember memini, isse + *gen*
remove (clothing) exuo, ere, ui, utum
repay reddo, ere, didi, ditum
repent paenitet + *acc of person, gen of thing repented of*
reply respondeo, ere, di, nsum
report nuntio [1]
republic res publica, rei publicae *f*
reputation fama, ae *f*; (good ~) existimatio, onis *f*; (bad ~) infamia, ae *f*
resist †re-sisto + *dat*
resolve censeo, ere, ui, sum; †con-stituo
respectable pudicus, a, um
rest *a*: the ~ *see pp. 53–4*
rest *n* quies, quietis *f*
rest *v* quiesco, ere, eui, etum
resting-place sepulcrum, i *n*
restore †re-stituo

return   (go back) *vi* †re-gredior; †red-eo;
  (give back) *vt* reddo, ere, didi, ditum
reveal   †pate-facio
revenge   ultio, onis *f*; get *or* take ~
  ulciscor, i, ultus sum
reward   praemium, ii *n*
rich   diues (*gen* ditis *or* diuitis)
riches   diuitiae, arum *f pl*; opes, um *f pl*
ride   equito [1]
right *n*   (in law) ius, iuris *n*; (in general)
  fas *n indecl*
right *a*: it is ~   decet, *see p. 76*
ring   anulus, i *m*
rise   †orior
rival   inimicus, a, um
river   flumen, inis *n*
roam   uagor [1]
rock   (large) saxum, i *n*; (smaller) lapis,
  idis *m*
roof   tectum, i *n*
room   conclaue, is *n*
rope   funis, is *m*
rose-bush   rosa, ae *f*
rule   †rego
run   †curro; ~ away (from) †fugio
rush   ruo, ere, ui, utum

sacred   sacer, cra, crum
sacrificial animal   uictima, ae *f*
sad   tristis, e
said: he/she ~   inquit
sail *v*   nauigo [1]
sail *n*: set ~   uelum †do
sailor   nauta, ae *m*
sake: for the ~ of   causa; gratia + *gen*
salesman   uenditor, is *m*
salt   sal, is *m*
same   idem, eadem, idem
savage   ferox (*gen* ocis)
save   seruo [1]
say   †dico; inquam *ir*; ~ ... not nego [1]
scary   horribilis, e; formidolosus, a, um
scheme   consilium, ii *n*
school   schola, ae *f*
scoundrel   nebulo, onis *m*
scout   explorator, is *m*
scream   clamo [1]
sculpt   sculpo, ere, psi, ptum

sculptor   sculptor, is *m*
sea   mare, is *n*
seal   †claudo
search party   exploratores, um *m pl*
second   secundus, a, um
secretary   scriba, ae *c*
secretly   furtim
see   †uideo; ~ to curo [1]
seed   semen, inis *n*
seek   †peto
seem   †uideor
seize   †capio; †rapio
self   ipse, a, um
self-evident   manifestus, a, um
sell   uendo, ere, didi, ditum
senate   senatus, us *m*
senate house   curia, ae *f*
senator   senator, is *m*
send   †mitto; ~ for arcesso, ere, iui, itum
sensible   sapiens (*gen* ntis)
serious   grauis, e
serpent   serpens, ntis *m/f*
serve   seruio [4] + *dat*
sesterce   sestertius, ii *m*
set out   (on journey) †proficiscor
settlement   uicus, i *m*
seven   septem
several   *see p. 52–3*
sew   suo, ere, sui, sutum
shadow   umbra, ae *f*
shame   pudor, is *m*; dedecus, oris *n*
shameless   impudicus, a, um
shamelessness   turpitudo, inis *f*
shepherd   pastor, is *m*
shine   luceo [2]
ship   nauis, is *f*
shipwright   naupegus, i *m*
shop *v*   (do the shopping) obsonor [1]
shore   litus, oris *n*
shout   clamo [1]; exclamo [1]
show *v*   ostendo, ere, di, nsum
show *n*   spectaculum, i *n*
shrine   sacrarium, ii *n*
sick: be ~   aegroto [1]
side: from every ~ undique; on this ~ of
  cis + *acc*
siege engine   ballista, ae *f*
sight: catch ~ of   †con-spicio

signal **signum, i** *n*

silent **tacitus, a, um; tacens** (*gen* ntis); remain ~ **taceo** [1]

silently **tacite**

silver *a* **argenteus, a, um**

silver *n* **argentum, i** *n*; piece of ~ (coin) **argenteus, i** *m*

since *c* *see pp. 80–84*

since *p* **post** + *acc*

sing †**cano**

sink *vi* **summergor, i, rsus sum**

sire **domine** (*voc*)

sister **soror, is** *f*

six **sex**

sixth **sextus, a, um**

skilled **peritus, a, um** (at/in + *gen*)

sky **caelum, i** *n*

slaughter †**caedo**

slave **seruus, i** *m*

sleep *n* **somnus, i** *m*

sleep *v* **dormio** [4]

slender **tenuis, e**

slip †**labor**; ~ away †**e-labor**

small **paruus, a, um**

smell *vi* **oleo** [2]; *vt* †**ol-facio**

smile at †**ad-rideo** + *dat*

smoke **fumus, i** *m*

snow *n* **nix, niuis** *f*

snow *v*: it ~s **ningit**

so (in such a way) **sic; ita**; (to such an extent) **tam** (+ *adj or adv*); **adeo** (+ *vb*); ~ many **tot** *indecl*; ~ big, great **tantus, a, um**; ~ often **totiens**; ~ that (in order that) *see p. 86–8*; ~ long as **dum (modo)**; and ~ **itaque**

soldier **miles, itis** *m*

some *see pp. 52–3*; ~ ... others **alii ... alii**

someone, something *see pp. 52–3*

son **filius, ii** *m* (*voc* mi fili)

soon **mox**

sorrow **dolor, is** *m*

sorry: be ~ **paenitet** + *acc of person*

sort: the ~ of *see p. 30*

sound **sono, are, ui, itum**

sow **sero, ere, seui, satum**

space (gap between) **interuallum, i** *n*

spare †**parco** + *dat*

sparkle **mico, are, cui**

speak †**loquor**

spear **hasta, ae** *f*

spectacle **spectaculum, i** *n*

speech **oratio, onis** *f*

speed **celeritas, atis** *f*

spend time **tempus** †**ago**

spin **neo, nere, neui, netum**

spirit (soul) **anima, ae** *f*; (ghost) **umbra, ae** *f*, **simulacrum, i** *n*; great ~ **magnanimitas, atis** *f*

spleen **splen, enis** *m*

spread †**dif-fundo**

sprite **umbra, ae** *f*

stable **stabulum, i** *n*

stag **ceruus, i** *m*

stage **proscaenium, ii** *n*

stand (bear) **tolero** [1]; ~ around †**circum-sto**

star **stella, ae** *f*

state **res publica, rei publicae** *f*

statue **statua, ae** *f*

stay †**maneo**

steady **firmus, a, um**

steal **aufero, ferre, abstuli, ablatum**

steward **uilicus, i** *m*

stick †**haereo**

still *c* **nihilominus; tamen**

still *adv* **etiamnunc; adhuc**

stone **lapis, idis** *m*

stop *vi* (cease) †**de-sino** + *infin*; (come to halt) †**con-sisto**; *vt* **prohibeo** [2]; **impedio** [4]

storm **tempestas, atis** *f*

story **fabula, ae** *f*

straightaway **statim**

strange **inusitatus, a, um; mirabilis, e**

stream **riuus, i** *m*

street **uia, ae** *f*

strength **uires, ium** *f pl*

strike **transfigo, ere, ixi**

struggle **certo** [1]

student **discipulus, i** *m*

study *n* (room) **tablinum, i** *n*; (pursuit) **studium, ii** *n*

study *v* **studeo** [2] + *dat*

stupid **stultus, a, um**

succeed **bene me** †**gero**

such **talis, e**

suddenly   subito; repente
suffer   †patior
suffocate   suffoco [1]
summer   aestas, atis *f*
summon   arcesso, ere, iui, itum
sun   sol, solis *m*
sunrise   solis ortus, us *m*
sunset   solis occasus, us *m*
supporter   adiutor, is *m*
sure   certus, a, um
surely ...?   nonne
surely ... not?   num
surprise: by ~   (ex *or* de) improuiso
surprising   mirus, a, um
surround   †circum-uenio
survive   †super-sum
suspicion   suspicio, onis *f*
suspicious: be ~   suspicor [1]
swear   adiuro [1]
sweet   dulcis, e
swift   *see* fast
swim   nato [1]
sword   gladius, ii *m*

table   mensa, ae *f*
talent   talentum, i *n*
talk   †loquor
tall   altus, a, um
take   (steal) aufero, ferre, abstuli,
   ablatum; (capture) †capio; (pick up)
   †sumo; ~ up (arms) †capio; ~ out †de-
   traho; ~ as wife uxorem †duco
task   negotium, ii *n*; opus, eris *n*; labor, is
   m
tasty   sapidus, a, um
tavern   taberna, ae *f*
tax   uectigalia, ium *n pl*
teach   doceo [2]
teacher   magister, tri *m*
tear *v*   (rip) scindo, ere, idi, issum
tear *n*   (of eyes) lacrima, ae *f*
tedious   molestus, a, um
tell   (say) †dico; (relate) narro [1];
   (inform) certiorem †facio; (order)
   †iubeo; impero [1] + *dat*
temple   templum, i *n*
tempt   allicio, ere, lexi, lectum
ten   decem

tent   (commander's ~) praetorium, ii *n*
terrible   atrox (*gen* ocis); terribilis, e
terrify   terreo [2]
test   experior, iri, ertus sum
thank   gratias †ago + *dat*
that *pron/adj*   ille, a, ud
that *c*   (introducing relative clause) qui,
   quae, quod; (indirect statement) *see*
   pp. 58–61; (fear clause) ne; (result
   clause) ut; *see also pp. 119–21*
theatre   theatrum, i *n*
then   tum; deinde
there   ibi; (to ~) eo; be ~ †ad-sum
therefore   ergo; igitur *usu second word*
thief   fur, is *m*; latro, onis *m*
thin   rarus, a, um
thing   res, rei *f*
think   puto [1]; arbitror [1]; existimo [1]
thirsty: be ~   sitio [4]
thirteen   tredecim
thirty   triginta
this   hic, haec, hoc
threaten   minor [1]
three   tres, ia; ~ times *a* triplex (*gen*
   plicis); *adv* ter
throne   (chair) sella, ae *f*; (kingdom)
   regnum, i *n*
through   per + *acc*
throw   †iacio; ~ back reicio, ere, ieci,
   ectum
thunderbolt   fulmen, inis *n*
tie up   †uincio
tilt   inclino [1]
time   tempus, oris *n*; at that ~ tum, tunc
tired   fessus, a, um
tired: be ~ of   taedet + *acc of person, gen of*
   thing
to   ad, in + *acc*; ~ and fro huc illuc
today   hodie
toga   toga, ae *f*
together   una
tomb   sepulcrum, i *n*
tongue   lingua, ae *f*
too   (also) et; quoque; ~ much nimis;
   many nimii, ae, a *pl*; ~ little parum
top: the ~ of   *use adj* summus, a, um
town   oppidum, i *n*
tragically   tragice

traitor **proditor, is** *m*
transparent **perspicuus, a, um**
trap **insidiae, arum** *f pl*
travel **peregrinor** [1]; **iter** †**facio**
traveller **peregrinator, is** *m*
treason **maiestas, atis** *f*
treasure (valuables) **opes, um** *f pl*; (booty) **praeda, ae** *f*
treat **tracto** [1]
tree **arbor, is** *f*
tremble **tremo, ere, ui**
trial **iudicium, ii** *n*
tribe **tribus, us** *f*
trim **nitidus, a, um**
tripod **tripus, podis** *m*
troops **copiae, arum** *f pl*
true **uerus, a, um**
trust †**credo** +*dat*
truth **uera** *n pl*; **quod uerum est** *n*
try **conor** [1]
tunic **tunica, ae** *f*
turn *vi* **retro uertor, i, rsus sum**; ~ out (end) **finior** [4]
twenty **uiginti** *indecl*
twice **bis**
twin **geminus, i** *m*
two **duo, ae**
typical: it is ~ of *use gen, see p. 8*
tyrant **tyrannus, i** *m*

unable: be ~ †**nequ-eo**; **non possum, posse, potui**
unaware **nescius, a, um**; be ~ of **nescio** [4]
unconscious **inanimus, a, um**
under **sub**; **subter** + *acc or abl*
understand †**intellego**
undetermined: be ~ (be undecided, hesitate) **dubito** [1]
undress = 'remove clothes'
unfinished **imperfectus, a, um**; **nondum perfectus, a, um**
unhappy **miser, era, erum**
unjust **iniustus, a, um**
unknowing **ignarus, a, um**
unknown **ignotus, a, um**; ~ to **clam** + *abl or acc*
unless **nisi**

unload †**de-pono**
unnoticed **praetermissus, a, um**
unsafe **periculosus, a, um**
unsuspecting = 'not suspicious'
until *see pp. 81–2*
unwilling: be ~ **nolo, nolle, nolui**
upset: become ~ †**com-moueor**
urge **hortor** [1]
urn **urna, ae** *f*
use †**utor** + *abl*
used to *use impf*; be ~ †**soleo** + *infin*
useful: be ~ †**pro-sum** + *dat*
usual: as ~ **ut fieri solet**
usurp **usurpo** [1]
utmost **summus, a, um**
utterly **prorsus**

vain: in ~ **nequiquam**; **frustra**
valley **ualles, is** *f*
verse **uersus, us** *m*
very *a* (self) **ipse, a, um**; (same) **idem, eadem, idem**
very *adv* **ualde**; *use superlative*
victor **uictor, is** *m*
view **uisus, us** *m*
villa **uilla, ae** *f*
village **uicus, i** *m*
visit **uisito** [1]
vivacity **alacritas, atis** *f*
vomit **uomo, ere, ui**

wait †**maneo**; ~ for **exspecto** [1]
wake **excito** [1]
walk **ambulo** [1]; **gradior, i**
wall **murus, i** *m*; town *or* city ~s **moenia, ium** *n pl*
wander **uagor** [1]; **erro** [1]
want †**uolo**; †**cupio**; (seek) †**peto**
war **bellum, i** *n*
warehouse **apotheca, ae** *f*
warn **moneo** [2]
warning **monitio, onis** *f*
warily **caute**; **circumspecte**
wash **lauo, are, laui**
water **aqua, ae** *f*
watch (guard) **custodio** [4]; (performance) **specto** [1]; (look on, at) †**a-spicio**
wax tablet **cera, ae** *f*

179

way: all the ~ to **usque ad** + *acc*; *abl or gen*
+ **tenus**; in this ~ **sic**; **ita**; in no ~ **nullo
modo**; **haudquaquam**
wealth *see* riches
wear (clothes) †**gero**; **induo, ere, ui,
utum**
weather **tempestas, atis** *f*
wedding **nuptiae, arum** *f pl*
weep **fleo** [2]
welcome *a* **expectatus, a, um**
welcome *v* †**ex-cipio**; **saluto** [1]
well *adv* **bene**
well *int* (in that case) **igitur**; **ergo**
what **quid**; **qui, quae, quod**; ~ a …! *see
p. 2*
wheel **rota, ae** *f*
when *see pp. 20–4, 60–3, 80–4*
whenever *see pp. 80–1, 83–4*
where **ubi**; ~ … from **unde**; ~ … to **quo**
whether **num**; ~ … or (ind. qn.) **utrum/-
ne … an**; (conditional) **seu/siue …
seu/siue**
which *see* who
while *c* *see pp. 80–4*
while *n*: for a little ~ **paullulum**
whip *v* **flagello** [1]
whip *n* **flagellum, i** *n*
whisper **susurro** [1]
who (in questions) *see p. 63*; (in rel.
clause) **qui, quae, quod**
whole **totus, a, um**
why **cur**; **quare**; **quamobrem**
wide **latus, a, um**
widow **uidua, ae** *f*
wife **uxor, is** *f*
wild beast **fera, ae** *f*
wily **callidus, a, um**
win †**uinco**
wind **uentus, i** *m*
window **fenestra, ae** *f*
winter **hiems, mis** *f*
wisdom **sapientia, ae** *f*

wise **sapiens** (*gen* **ntis**)
with **cum** + *abl*
wither **languesco, ere, ui**
without **sine** + *abl*
witness **testis, is** *m*
wolf **lupus, i** *m*
woman **femina, ae** *f*; **mulier, is** *f*
wonder *v* (be amazed) **miror** [1]; (want
to know) **scire** †**uolo**; (be uncertain)
dubito [1]
wonder *n* **miraculum, i** *n*
wonderful **mirus, a, um**
wood (area with trees) **silua, ae** *f*; (fire~)
ligna, orum *n pl*; (timber) **materia, ae** *f*
word **uerbum, i** *n*
work *n* **labor, is** *m*; **opus, eris** *n*
work *v* **laboro** [1]
world **orbis terrarum** *m*; the next ~
Elysium, ii *n*
worried **commotus, a, um**
worship †**colo**
worthy **dignus, a, um** (of + *abl*)
wound *n* **uulnus, eris** *n*
wound *v* **uulnero** [1]
wretched **perditus, a, um**; **miser, era,
erum**
write †**scribo**
writer **auctor, is** *m*; **scriptor, is** *m*; **scriba,
ae** *m*
wrong *n* (in general) **nefas** *n indecl*
wrongly (mistakenly) **falso**

year **annus, i** *m*
yellow **luteus, a, um**; **flauus, a, um**
yesterday **heri**
yet: not ~ **nondum**
young **adulescens** (*gen* **ntis**); (little)
paruulus, a, um; ~ person **adulescens,
ntis** *c*; **iuuenis, is** *c*; ~ woman (girl)
puella, ae *f*; ~ man (boy) **puer, eri** *m*
your (sg) **tuus, a, um**
youth: from his ~ **a puero**

Proper names

Acilius **Acilius, ii** *m*
Acme **Acme, es** *f*

Acropolis **arx, arcis** *f*
Actium **Actium, ii** *n*

Aeneas **Aeneas, ae** *m*
Aeschylus **Aeschylus, i** *m*
Africa **Africa, ae** *f*; African **Africus, a, um**
Agrippina **Agrippina, ae** *f*
Alexandria **Alexandria, ae** *f*
Alcibiades **Alcibiades, is** *m*
Antiochus **Antiochus, i** *m*
Antium **Antium, ii** *n*
Antony **Antonius, ii** *m*
Apollo **Apollo, inis** *m*
Arab(ian) **Arabicus, a, um**
Ariamnes **Ariamnes, is** *m*
Ariovistus **Ariouistus, i** *m*
Arpinum **Arpinum, i** *n*
Asia **Asia, ae** *f*
Atalanta **Atalanta, ae** *f*
Athens **Athenae, arum** *f pl*; Athenian **Atheniensis, e**
Atticus **Atticus, i** *m*
Aulus **Aulus, i** *m*
Azora **Azora, ae** *f*

Baiae **Baiae, arum** *f pl*
Balbus **Balbus, i** *m*
Boudicca **Boudicca, ae** *f*
Britain **Britannia, ae** *f*; Briton **Britannus, i** *m*
Brutus **Brutus, i** *m*

Cador **Cador, is** *m*
Caecilius **Caecilius, ii** *m*
Caesar **Caesar, is** *m*
Candaules **Candaules, is** *m* (*acc* **en**)
Capitol **Capitolium, ii** *n*
Capua **Capua, ae** *f*
Carthage **Carthago, inis** *f*; Carthaginian **Carthaginiensis, e**
Cato **Cato, onis** *m*
Catullus **Catullus, i** *m*
Cerberus **Cerberus, i** *m*
Charybdis **Charybdis, is** *f*
Cicero **Cicero, onis** *m*
Cincinnatus **Cincinnatus, i** *m*
Circus Maximus **Circus Maximus, i** *m*
Cleopatra **Cleopatra, ae** *f*
Clodia **Clodia, ae** *f*
Clodius **Clodius, ii** *m*
Corcyra **Corcyra, ae** *f*
Corinna **Corinna, ae** *f*

Corinth **Corinthus, i** *f*
Coriolanus **Coriolanus, i** *m*
Cornelia **Cornelia, ae** *f*
Crassus **Crassus, i** *m*
Cumae **Cumae, arum** *f pl*
Cupid **Cupido, inis** *m*
Cynthia **Cynthia, ae** *f*

Dascylus **Dascylus, i** *m*
Decimus **Decimus, i** *m*
Delphi **Delphi, orum** *m pl*
Dido **Dido, onis** *f*
Dionysus **Dionysus, i** *m*

Egypt **Aegyptus, i** *f*; Egyptian **Aegyptius, a, um**
Ennius **Ennius, ii** *m*
Epaphroditus **Epaphroditus, i** *m*
Europe: of ~ **Europaeus, a, um**

Fabius **Fabius, ii** *m*
Falco **Falco, onis** *m*
Faustus **Faustus, i** *m*
Formiae: at ~ **Formianus, a, um**
Fortunata **Fortunata, ae** *f*
Furies **Furiae, arum** *f pl*

Gaius **Gaius, ii** *m*
Gaul **Gallia, ae** *f*; of ~ **Gallus, a, um**
Greece **Graecia, ae** *f*; Greek **Graecus, a, um**
Gyges **Gyges, is** *m* (*voc* **a**, *acc* **en**)

Hannibal **Hannibal, alis** *m*
Hispala **Hispala, ae** *f*
Homer **Homerus, i** *m*
Horace **Horatius, ii** *m*
Hyrcanian **Hyrcanus, a, um**

Iceni **Iceni, orum** *m pl*
Italy **Italia, ae** *f*

Julia **Iulia, ae** *f*
Jupiter **Iuppiter, Iouis** *m*

Latin **Latinus, a, um**; ~ language **lingua Latina**; in ~ **Latine**
Lesbia **Lesbia, ae** *f*
Leucas **Leucas, adis**
Livia **Liuia, ae** *f*
Livy **Liuius, ii** *m*
London **Londinium, ii** *n*

181

Lucius   **Lucius, ii** *m*
Lucretius   **Lucretius, ii** *m*

Macbeth: Lady ~   **Domina Macbeth**
Manius   **Manius, ii** *m*
Marius   **Marius, ii** *m*
Mark   **Marcus, i** *m*
Medusa   **Medusa, ae** *f*
Menander   **Menander, dri** *m*
Mettius   **Mettius, ii** *m*
Milo   **Milo, onis** *m*
Minerva   **Minerua, ae** *f*

Naples   **Neapolis, is** *f* (*acc* im)
Nausicaa   **Nausicaa, ae** *f*
Neptune   **Neptunus, i** *m*
Nero   **Nero, onis** *m*

Octavius   **Octauius, ii** *m*
Olympic Games   **ludi Olympiaci, orum** *m pl*
Orestes   **Orestes, is** *m* (*voc* a)
Orpheus   **Orpheus, ei** *m*
Ovid   **Ouidius, ii** *m*

Parthian   **Parthus, a, um**
Paula   **Paula, ae** *f*
Persian   **Persa, ae** *m*
Pharnabazus   **Pharnabazus, i** *m*
Philip   **Philippus, i** *m*
Pisa   **Pisa, ae** *f*
Plautus   **Plautus, i** *m*; of Plautus **Plautinus, a, um**
Pliny   **Plinius, ii** *m*
Pluto   **Pluto, onis** *m*
Po: around the River ~   **Circumpadanus, a, um**
Polyphemus   **Polyphemus, i** *m*
Pompeii   **Pompeii, orum** *m pl*; Pompeian **Pompeianus, a, um**
Pompey   **Pompeius, ii** *m*
Propertius   **Propertius, ii** *m*
Psyche   **Psyche, es** *f* (*voc* e, *acc* en, *dat* ae, *abl* e)
Publius   **Publius, ii** *m*
Pythian   (oracle) **Pythia, ae** *f*

Quintus   **Quintus, i** *m*

Regulus   **Regulus, i** *m*
Rome   **Roma, ae** *f*; Roman **Romanus, a, um**
Romulus   **Romulus, i** *m*
Rufilla   **Rufilla, ae** *f*
Rufus   **Rufus, i** *m*

Sardis   **Sardes, ium** *f pl*
Scipio   **Scipio, onis** *m*
Scylla   **Scylla, ae** *f*
Scythians   **Scythae, arum** *m pl*
Septimius   **Septimius, i** *m*
Servius   **Seruius, ii** *m*
Setoc   **Setox, ocis** *m*
Sextus   **Sextus, i** *m*
Sirmio   **Sirmio, onis** *f*
Socrates   **Socrates, is** *m*
Spanish, Spaniard   **Hispanus, a, um**
Spartacus   **Spartacus, i** *m*
Stentor   **Stentor, is** *m*
Stephanus   **Stephanus, i** *m*
Sulpicia   **Sulpicia, ae** *f*
Syracuse   **Syracusae, arum** *f pl*

Tacitus   **Tacitus, i** *m*
Tarquin   **Tarquinius, ii** *m*
Terence   **Terentius, ii** *m*; of Terence **Terentianus, a, um**
Titus   **Titus, i** *m*
Tiro   **Tiro, onis** *m*
Trajan   **Traianus, i** *m*
Troy   **Troia, ae** *f*; Trojans **Troes, um** *m pl*
Tullia   **Tullia, ae** *f*
Tuscan, Tusculan   **Tusculanus, a, um**

Ulysses   **Vlixes, is** *m*
Underworld   **Tartarus, i** *m*

Valerius   **Valerius, ii** *m*
Varus   **Varus, i** *m*
Venus   **Venus, eris** *f*
Verona   **Verona, ae** *f*
Verres   **Verres, is** *m*
Vesuvius   **Vesuuius, ii** *m*
Virgil   **Vergilius, ii** *m*

Zadig   **Zadigus, i** *m*

Index

Where an entry or subentry for a topic has more than one reference, we highlight its main discussion in **bold** face.

Index

neque, *see* nec
nescioquis 53
neu, neue 68–70, 86, 144–5
nisi 55, **90–3**
noli, nolite 68
nominative 1, 78, 140
non 90, 97, 99, 117, 119–20, 136
Nones, Nonae 158
nonne 64
nonnulli 52
nos 49
num 55, 64–5
numerals:
  cardinal 33, **155–6**
  ordinal 55–6, **156**, 158
  distributive 157
numquam 16, 55
nusquam 18

o:
  with vocative 1
  with accusative 2
oportet 76–7
opus est 12
or 65, 93, 128
oratio obliqua, see reported speech
ordinal numbers, *see* numerals
other, others 53–4

participles 11, **20–24**, 129, 137, 144
  see also under individual tenses
passive verbs 21, 75, 107
past sequence **45**, 46, 65, 104–7
penalty 9
per 15, **35**, 76–7
perfect tense:
  indicative 42, 80
  subjunctive 45, 46, 68, 96, 105, 134
  participle 21–2, 23
  reported statement 65
peritus 110–11

personal pronouns **49–50**, 123, 125
persuadeo 4, 71, 77
place 16–18
  where 11, 16
  from where 17
  to where 17
pluperfect tense:
  indicative 42, 81
  subjunctive 45, 46, 105, 106–7
plus 7
possessives 50–1
possum 43, 92
post 15, 35
postpositions 9, 38, 111
postquam 80–1
praecipio 4, 71
predicative dative 5
prepositions **33–7**, 125
  with accusative 35–7
  with ablative 33–4
present sequence **45–6**, 65, 104–7
present tense:
  indicative 41, 43, 82
    historic use **137**, 143
  subjunctive 45, 46, 65, 69, 96, 105, 106
  participle 20–1, 137
preventing, verbs of 119–21
price 11
pridie 14, 158
primary sequence, *see* present sequence
primum 80
pro 10, 33, 139
prohibeo 121
pronouns 49–56
  personal 49–50, 141
  demonstrative 51, 52
  reflexive 50, 54
proper names, *see* names
provided that 82
purpose ('final') clauses **86–8**, 144–5
  using relative 29
  future pple 24

qualis 28, 66
quam 12, 30, 66
quamdiu 66, 80–1
quamquam 100–1
quamuis 100–1
quando 55, 80 n. 1, 86, 92
quantus 28, 66
quare 66
quasi 101–2
quater 156–7
-que 125, 127
quemadmodum 66
questions **63–6**, 90, 104, 125, 150
qui **26–30**, 52, 53, 54, 63
quia 99–100
quid 52, 55, 66, 86, 92
quidam 52–3
quidem 126
quilibet 55
quin 113, **119–20**, 121
quippe **29**, 100
quis 52, 55, 86, 92, 138
quisquam **55**, 61, 127, 138
quisque 55–6
quiuis 55
quo 18, 28, 66, 87, 99, 146
quo modo 99
quoad 81–2
quod 52, 99–100
quod si 92
quominus **120–1**, 134
quoniam 99–100
quot 28, 66
quotie(n)s 28, 66, 80–1

reflexives, *see* pronouns
relative clauses **26–30**, 52, 53, 54, 138
  expressing kind 30, 53
  expressing purpose 29, 87
  expressing result 30
  expressing cause 29
  connecting relative **28–9**, 134, 137, 140, 146
relinquo 17
reliqui 53–4
remote conditions, *see* hypothetical conditions

185